Popular Mechanics

MoneySmart Makeovers
Kitchens

Rick Peters

HEARST BOOKS

A division of Sterling Publishing Co., Inc.

New York / London
www.sterlingpublishing.com

Every effort has been made to ensure that all the information in this book is accurate. However, due to differing conditions, tools, and individual skills, the publisher cannot be responsible for any injuries, losses, and/or other damages that may result from the use of the information in this book.

Produced by Rick Peters, Hackettstown, NJ
Design: Sandy Freeman/Cover design: Celia Fuller
Photography: Christopher J. Vendetta
Front cover photo: courtesy of Bosch Appliances
Back cover photos: courtesy of Timberlake Cabinet Company
Contributing writer: Cheryl Romano
Illustrations: Bob Crimi
Copy Editor: Barbara McIntosh Webb
Page layout: Sandy Freeman
Index: Nan Badgett

Safety Note: Homes built prior to 1978 may have been constructed with hazardous materials: lead and asbestos. You can test painted surfaces with a test kit available at most hardware stores. Asbestos can be found in ceiling and wall materials, joint compound, insulation, and flooring. Hire a professional, licensed hazardous-removal company to check for this and remove any hazardous materials found.

Page 1 photo courtesy of Timberlake Cabinet Company

Library of Congress catalogued the hardcover edition as follows:
Peters, Rick.
    Kitchens : moneysmart makeovers /Rick Peters.
        p. cm.
    At head of title: Popular mechanics.
    Includes index.
    ISBN 1-58816-255-9
    1. Kitchens--Remodeling. I. Popular mechanics. II. Title

TH4816.3.K58P47 2004
643.3—dc22

2003060555

10 9 8 7 6 5 4 3 2 1

First Paperback Edition 2007
Published by Hearst Books
A Division of Sterling Publishing Co., Inc.
387 Park Avenue South, New York, NY 10016

Popular Mechanics and Hearst Books are trademarks of Hearst Communications, Inc.

www.popularmechanics.com

For information about custom editions, special sales, premium and corporate purchases, please contact Sterling Special Sales Department at 800-805-5489 or specialsales@sterlingpub.com.

Distributed in Canada by Sterling Publishing
c/o Canadian Manda Group, 165 Dufferin Street
Toronto, Ontario, Canada M6K 3H6

Distributed in Australia by Capricorn Link (Australia) Pty. Ltd.
P.O. Box 704, Windsor, NSW 2756 Australia

Manufactured in China

Sterling ISBN 13: 978-1-58816-670-8
     ISBN 10: 1-58816-670-8

Acknowledgments

For all their help, advice, and support, I offer special thanks to:

Connie Edwards, CKD, CKB, Director of Design at Timberlake Cabinet Company, and Tessa Bull (also from Timberlake)—consummate professionals—for their unstinting assistance and much-valued design know-how.

Randy Hicks, National Sales Manager for Quality Doors, for the materials used for refacing the cabinets in the mid-range makeover.

Vanessa Trost of Identiteam for the ultra-chic and extremely well designed Gaggenau appliances installed in the high-end makeover.

Don Nordmeyer of DuPont and Annemarie Armentano of Porter-Novelli for the beautiful Corian and Zodiaq countertops used in the mid-range and high-end makeovers.

Amy Christiansen of Burton Luch for the incredibly quiet Bosch dishwasher installed in the high-end makeover.

Jana Rhodes and Julie Skowland of Walt Denny, Inc., for the high-quality Amerock hardware used for the cabinets in all three kitchen makeovers.

Rob Jenkins of Rev-a-Shelf for storage accessories.

Linda Bendt of Always Thinking for the well-crafted Danze faucets for the economy and mid-range makeovers.

Dean Springmeyer and Don Kresker of US Kitchens for their expertise and advice in design and installation.

Joe Pyskaty and Todd Nykun, craftsmen and cabinet installers, for cabinet installation within a tight deadline, and with constant stops for photography.

Al D'Alessandro of Marvic and his ace crew of countertop installers: Cosimo Orsillo, Francisco Vasquez, Michael Sialer, Jimmy Pinto, and Alex McGarry.

Christopher Vendetta, for taking great photographs.

Sandy Freeman, book designer extraordinaire, whose exquisite art talents are evident on every page of this book.

Bob Crimi, for superb illustrations.

Barb Webb, copyediting whiz, for ferreting out mistakes and gently suggesting corrections.

Heartfelt thanks to my constant inspiration: Cheryl, Lynne, Will, and Beth.

Contents

Photo courtesy of American Woodmark

Introduction

Make over a kitchen? It happens every day; the bookshelves are full of examples of taking one room, making some changes, and...Ta-daaa! There's your makeover. One "before," one "after," and you're done. This book is different.

We take one real kitchen and make it over not once, not twice, but three times to demonstrate what you can do in the real world with real budgets. Everyone appreciates the "beauty" shots in print and broadcast media, but most of these are set up in studios with phony props, professional set decorators, and sky-high price tags. In this book, every project was started and finished in a real kitchen, used every day by a family of four (plus two dogs).

Photo courtesy of Moen

Unlike those single-version makeovers, we show you the same kitchen, revamped three times, to demonstrate what you can do on a budget: economy, mid-range, and high-end. Want to mix and match from all three makeovers? Love one particular version and want to duplicate it in your home? We show you how.

MoneySmart Makeovers: Kitchens is divided into three parts to help you get the kitchen you want.

First, the "Planning Your Makeover" section covers the important—but sometimes overlooked—fundamentals you need to know. Then, "Real Makeover Examples" shows you our real-life kitchen so you can see the results of three different spending levels. Finally, "Creating Your New Look" guides you through the nuts-and-bolts basics that show you how to tackle each project, one step at a time.

MoneySmart Makeovers: Kitchens is the only guide you'll need to achieve the kitchen you want, with the budget you have.

The Editors of *Popular Mechanics*

Planning Your Makeover

If an upgraded kitchen is your destination, how do you get there? This section is your road map to get you familiar with the terrain along the way.

We'll look at basics of kitchen design, choosing materials, and kitchen systems (plumbing, electrical, etc.). Separately and together, they're all essential parts of mapping out your makeover. There's a lot more involved here than a coat of paint and new drawer pulls. Everything in a kitchen—the cooking units, the countertop material, the location of a door—affects all the other elements. Consider this: You replace your old appliances with spiffy new ones, and now the cabinets, floor, and walls look dreary (in fact, that's a common impetus for a makeover).

Because there are so many aspects to a kitchen—traffic patterns, function, appearance, and, of course, budget—you need to consider the whole room, not just one part.

The point is, don't rush off to the home center without a complete plan, or destination. The chapters in this section will help you get there.

photo courtesy of Timberlake Cabinet Company

KITCHEN DESIGN

In fantasyland, kitchens are as big as parking lots, cost six figures–plus, and merely look fabulous—no one actually cooks in them. Your kitchen, though, is probably closer to 12 × 12 and really gets used, and your budget is four, maybe five figures. That's why you need to think over your makeover before you fall in love with a picture and dash out to start buying.

It's one thing to paint a bedroom for an entirely new look. But a kitchen is the most complicated room in the house, and what you do with one part can affect all the others. Plumbing, electricity, lighting, storage, traffic patterns … these separate elements all have to be considered.

To be money-smart and just plain smart about your makeover, identify your goal (more counter space, for example), assess what you have, and plan the choices that will achieve your best result. Think of this as the reality-check section: This is where the realities of your own lifestyle, space, and budget will shape your new, really improved kitchen.

KITCHEN STYLES

■ With so many changes involved, where do you begin? Choosing a style for your kitchen is one of the best ways to organize a makeover. As soon as you decide on a style, many of the other design possibilities are eliminated, leaving you with a much more manageable array of choices. There are many distinctive styles or themes to select from, the most popular being Arts & Crafts, Retro, Modern, Country, Shaker, Contemporary, and Architectural. The makeover police aren't on duty, so mix and match at will to create your own style.

Arts & Crafts. Kitchens based on the Arts & Crafts movement (also called Mission or Craftsman style) feature plain wood cabinets with minimal decoration (right). Windows are curtainless to allow the light to flood the space. Countertops are often natural stone, and walls are painted with warm colors, such as the yellow shown here. Mission-style lighting and iron hardware help polish the look.

Retro. This style (below) has become "hot" in recent years as homeowners strive to recreate kitchens of the past. The two versions that are the most prevalent are early American, like the kitchen shown here, and '50s-style retro. The key to both looks is finding appliances to match the period. Cabinets are often painted light, pastel colors.

Photo courtesy of Timberlake Cabinet Company

Photo courtesy of Heartland Appliances

Photo courtesy of Timberlake Cabinet Company

Photo courtesy of Timberlake Cabinet Company

Photo courtesy of American Woodmark

Modern. With a modern- or European-style kitchen, the emphasis is on architectural shapes and a strong linear interior (top left). The cabinets are natural woods or painted (as shown here) and are often unadorned. In most cases, the cabinets are full overlay (see page 28) and are often edged with a contrasting material. Walls are adorned with geometric patterns, and bold colors are key accents.

Country. Country kitchens (top right) create a "back at the farm" feel, even if the setting is a high-rise condo. Soft-edged accents with plenty of curves are predominant, such as the window treatment shown here. Walls are typically wallpapered with a flower design or border, setting off cabinets of oak or maple with curved doors. Farm sinks are common and are usually porcelain or cast iron.

Shaker. Elegantly simple, a Shaker kitchen (left) embraces the Shaker philosophy of "less is more." Clean lines and minimal decoration create an uncluttered space that many find calming. Natural woods and pastel colors work well with this style.

KITCHEN STYLES,
continued

Contemporary. Strong horizontal elements and clean lines typify a contemporary kitchen (right). This eclectic style often combines high-tech surfaces and appliances with handmade accessories such as lighting and hardware. Accents are often bold and can be chrome, ceramic, glass, steel, or brass.

Photo courtesy of Merillat

Photo courtesy of Wellborn Cabinets

Architectural. An architectural kitchen (left) offers a more formal and dignified feel by using classic forms of the past. Columns and turned posts are used to support cabinets and countertops, in addition to serving as decoration. Windows, doors, and ceilings are often treated with elaborate moldings. Delicate and patterned tiles serve as excellent accents to this refined style.

SPECIALTY AREAS

Desk space. A space for cookbooks, recipes, and possibly a computer is one of the most asked-for specialty areas in the kitchen. The cabinets at left in the photo create an efficient, well-organized location for all these.

Photo courtesy of American Woodmark

Baking. For cooks who bake, there's nothing like a special area expressly for this activity. A marble countertop complements the cabinets, and its cool surface is perfect for kneading and rolling dough and making pastries.

Photo courtesy of Canac

ISLANDS AND PENINSULAS

Photo courtesy of KitchenAid

Photo courtesy of Wellborn Cabinet

■ Three of the most common complaints people have about their kitchens are: not enough storage, too little counter space, and no place for seating. The remedy to all of these is a kitchen island or peninsula. Both provide plenty of storage, lots more counter area for food preparation, and, if you extend the top out a bit, a cozy spot for a couple of chairs or stools.

Island. If your kitchen space allows, an island (top) placed in the center is your best bet—just make sure there's adequate walkway clearance all around it and that the island doesn't interfere with work flow (see page 14). If you plan the placement of the island right, it should improve work flow; you may even want to consider installing a cooktop, a full sink, or a small prep sink in the island to make the kitchen more efficient.

Snack bars. If your kitchen is too small for either an island or a peninsula, you can still have an eating area with a snack bar (middle). This can be accomplished by simply extending a countertop over a cabinet edge, as shown here. Another option is to mount a length of countertop to an unused wall (see page 118). If you've got a tiny space, like a corridor kitchen, you can hinge the counter to drop down when not in use.

Peninsula. A peninsula (bottom) works well in smaller kitchens where an island would hamper work flow. A peninsula is a great way to provide an eating area in the kitchen without taking up much space. Here again, you can install a cooktop or sink in it; if you do, consider raising the countertop for the eating area to separate it from the kitchen as we did in the high-end kitchen shown on pages 56–58.

Work Flow and Traffic Patterns

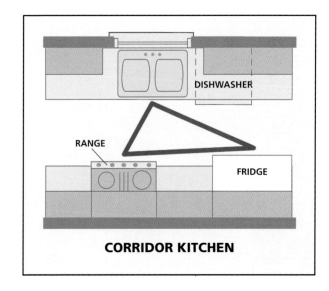

CORRIDOR KITCHEN

■ It's amazing how many kitchens are designed without giving thought to the cook. Sure, they might be gorgeous to look at, but will a cook truly enjoy working in the space? One of the biggest factors that affects this is the work flow. That is, how a meal flows from start to finish, from pulling the ingredients out of the refrigerator and pantry to setting the table. In years past, only three parts of the process were considered: the refrigerator, the sink, and the range. These three constitute the work triangle that is still used in kitchen design today.

The National Kitchen & Bath Association (NKBA; see page 15) recommends that no single side of the triangle be more than 9 feet, and that the combined length of the sides not exceed 26 feet. But in today's kitchens the "triangle" is more like a polygon: cooktop, sink, refrigerator, wall oven, microwave...you get the idea. The best way to see whether a kitchen layout will work for you is to mentally "rehearse" cooking a meal or two in it. Think about your steps, from start to finish. Odds are you'll find that you keep bumping into something, or that you have to walk around an island or peninsula too much. Alter the design as necessary to remedy such faults.

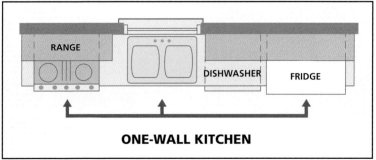

ONE-WALL KITCHEN

Work flow depends primarily on the layout of the kitchen. We've illustrated six of the most common layouts here, along with their work triangles. Traffic patterns—how you move through the kitchen—will be affected by the location of the kitchen in the home, and by the surrounding rooms. Keep in mind that if you alter the work flow in the kitchen—say, by adding an island—you'll likely alter the traffic flow; try not to hinder traffic patterns at the cost of better work flow.

Corridor kitchen. For a single cook, a corridor kitchen can be quite efficient as long as the work centers are grouped close together. The big disadvantage of this plan is that household traffic usually must flow through the space as well.

One-wall kitchen. The least efficient kitchen plan, a one-wall kitchen has all the work centers placed along a single wall. These are necessities in efficiency apartments or studios. One advantage is that they can be concealed with sliding or folding doors.

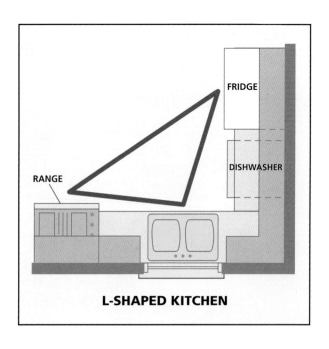

L-SHAPED KITCHEN

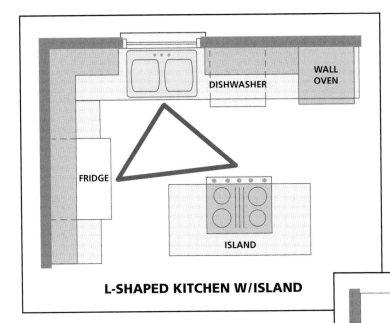

L-SHAPED KITCHEN W/ISLAND

L-shaped kitchen. Generous counter space is the biggest advantage of an L-shaped plan. Care must be taken to group the work centers together; otherwise, you have an elongated work triangle that creates many wasted steps.

L-shaped with island. By adding a free-standing island to an L-shaped kitchen, you can tighten up the work triangle as well as increase storage space. An extended countertop on the island can also provide seating for an eating area.

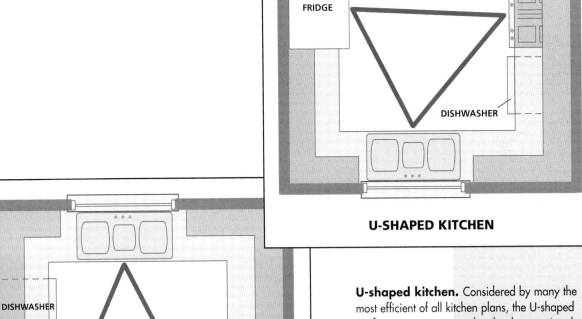

U-SHAPED KITCHEN

G-SHAPED KITCHEN

U-shaped kitchen. Considered by many the most efficient of all kitchen plans, the U-shaped configuration saves steps by closely grouping the work centers. The cook is also surrounded by plenty of countertop and storage space.

G-shaped kitchen. A derivative of the U-shape, the G-shaped plan adds an extra wall of cabinets and countertop that wrap around to become a peninsula. The only disadvantage to this layout is that it can give the kitchen an enclosed feeling.

KITCHEN PLANNING

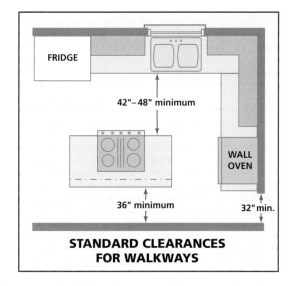

STANDARD CLEARANCES FOR WALKWAYS

■ The first step in planning a makeover is to determine your budget. Ask yourself what you can afford to spend, and answer honestly. If you're after a major makeover, consider a home equity loan or other financing. Once you've identified what you can spend, zero in on the look you're after. Clip photos out from magazines and collect samples of fabric, wall coverings, and surfaces that might go with the plan. This is helpful whether you're getting professional design help (see the sidebar below) or choosing everything yourself. If money is tight, splurge on just a single item, like a solid-surface countertop or a new refrigerator.

General design guidelines. The NKBA (see the sidebar on page 15) has published a set of design guidelines for creating successful kitchens. Although there are 40 guidelines (some very technical), a more general, shorter list is shown below to help you plan.

1. There should be at least one triangle in place.
2. The lengths of the sides of the triangle combined should not exceed 26 feet.
3. Traffic flow shouldn't interfere with the triangle; neither should islands or peninsulas.
4. Make sure there's at least 3 feet of countertop space in the mixing/food preparation area.

5. The counter should be at least 9" wide on one side and at least 15" on the other side of a cooktop.
6. For the sink, the counter should be at least 18" wide on one side and at least 24" on the other side.
7. Create a staging area for the oven—a spot where you can place a roast or casserole while you open or close the door: a 15"-wide counter on one side of a built-in oven or on an island that's no more than 48" from the oven.
8. A refrigerator should also have a 15"-wide counter space that's no more than 48" from the refrigerator.
9. The dishwasher should be within 36" of the sink.
10. Try to leave at least 21" between the dishwasher and nearby appliances or counters to allow for loading and unloading.
11. Plan for at least 12" to 19" of leg room under eating areas in islands, peninsulas, etc.
12. Create as much accessible storage space as possible.
13. Make the aisles wide enough for two people to pass each other (see the drawing above).
14. Provide plenty of overall lighting, and don't forget task lighting at the sink, range, and prep areas.

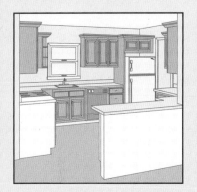

WORKING WITH A KITCHEN DESIGNER

■ If new cabinets are part of your makeover, consider getting professional help—even if you plan on installing the cabinets yourself. For starters, a kitchen designer has access to all major cabinet manufacturers and will know which is best for you. Next, they'll ask you questions about how you cook, size of family, etc. Then, given your budget and space limitations, they'll design your kitchen. Most designers use high-tech drafting programs, so they can show you exactly what your new kitchen will look like. What's really nice is that they can change details (such as cabinet style) with a single click—even adding or subtracting a cabinet is no big deal. Finally, they'll be able to generate an order list that will specify everything you need, from crown molding to filler strips.

Measuring a kitchen. If your makeover calls for new cabinets or countertops, you'll want to start by making a rough sketch of your kitchen. The grids on graph paper will help make it accurate. Start by measuring the kitchen from wall to wall on each wall, and record these dimensions on your sketch. Since few homes are ever square, it's best to measure in three places: at the floor, midway up the wall, and at the ceiling. Measure and record the ceiling height and then pencil in the windows and doors; include which way the doors open. (See the section below on measuring windows and doors accurately.) Then locate the centerline on your sink and note this on your drawing. Note the distance from the corner of the sink to this centerline. Then mark the locations of the existing electrical receptacles and any light fixtures. Take this sketch with you when you speak with a designer or anytime you have parts custom-ordered.

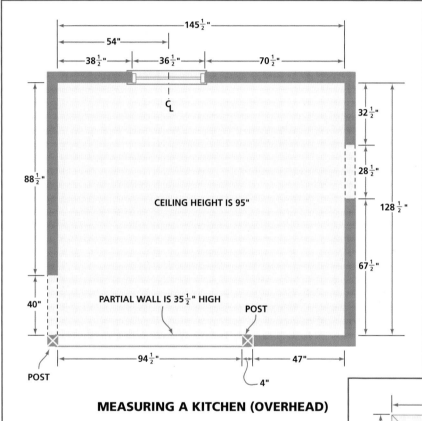

MEASURING A KITCHEN (OVERHEAD)

THE NKBA

■ The National Kitchen & Bath Association is a nonprofit trade association that has educated and led the kitchen and bath industry for more than 35 years.

NKBA helps consumers by acting as the ultimate resource for everything from finding a design professional in your area to providing updates on industry trends, products, and services. They publish a free consumer workbook that offers remodeling tips and guides you through the process of redesigning your kitchen or bath from beginning to end. Visit their site at www.nkba.org for more information.

Measuring windows and doors. Incorrectly measuring windows and doors is one of the most common mistakes a homeowner can make when planning a kitchen upgrade. The frequent mistake? Measuring the inside dimensions. But this doesn't take into account the trim. To measure a window or door correctly, measure from the outside trim to the outside trim and record these dimensions on your floor plan.

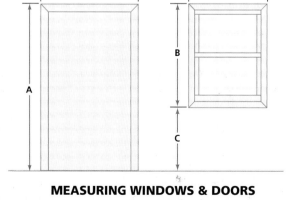

MEASURING WINDOWS & DOORS

WINDOWS AND DOORS

■ One of the most often overlooked, but highly visible, makeover techniques in a kitchen is to enhance the windows or doors. This can be as simple as new window treatments or as complex as replacing a small door with a sliding patio door.

For limited budgets, new trim (see page 146) and custom micro-shades can do wonders. For the more adventurous, consider upgrading the window if it's old and tired (especially if it's a single-pane window that offers virtually no insulation properties) with a vinyl replacement window with double panes and maybe even divided sections. Alternatively, you can dress up a standard window with retrofit muntins—these are self-adhesive and simply attach to the windowpanes.

If replacing a window yourself makes you nervous, you can get a new one installed for a modest fee. Many home centers now offer this service, or check your phone book listings under Windows, Replacement.

Photo courtesy of Hy-Lite Products, Inc.

Photo courtesy of Heartland Appliances

If you're an experienced do-it-yourselfer, you can make a dramatic change in the look and feel of a kitchen by installing a larger window. Just keep in mind that if the window is over the sink, odds are that the vent wraps around the window and you'll need to reroute it; see page 43 for more on this.

Door replacement is a fairly straightforward task that can also have a great impact on the kitchen. Imagine going from a solid exterior door to a full-view metal and glass door—just think about all that beautiful light flowing into the kitchen! Because kitchen doors get a lot of use, make sure you purchase a brand name you can depend on.

STORAGE

PULL-OUT UNITS

Waste containers. A direct pull-out is the most efficient available—and that's essential for waste containers that are constantly opened and closed.

Recycling. For larger bins, like the recycling unit here, double doors are needed to handle the wider containers—one each for glass, plastic, and metal.

Wire racks. Pull-out wire racks are a handy way to store pots, pans, dry goods, and even produce such as onions and potatoes.

■ There are a number of ways to increase storage space in the kitchen. A new arrangement of cabinets and the addition of an island or peninsula (see page 11) are just a couple.

If your plans don't allow for this, the next best alternative is to maximize the space you have. Cabinet and cabinet accessory manufacturers sell units that can turn unused space (like the unreachable back section of a corner cabinet) into useable space. Tilt-out bins (see page 92) and pull-out bins (see the sidebar at left) are other nifty ways you can squeeze more storage out of a small space. Even simple organizing units that drop into drawers can help; the better organized and more efficient a kitchen is, the more space you'll have for storage.

Lazy Susans. A lazy Susan is a quick way to increase storage space in a corner cabinet (near left). They are available in full circles, D-shape, pie-cut, and half-moon shapes (as shown here). They typically attach to the cabinet via a pair of upper and lower brackets. Installation is simple and quick. .

Drawer organizers. You can maximize your drawer storage space by inserting organizers like the one shown here (top). Some accessory manufacturers make rolling tray systems that let you stack trays on top of each other; they roll back and forth to provide full access to contents below.

LIGHTING

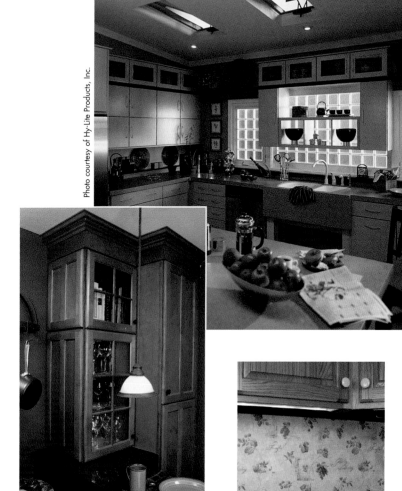

■ On a small budget, one of the most dramatic ways you can make over a kitchen is with lighting. It's amazing how different a kitchen can look and feel by going from a single overhead fixture to several well-placed lighting elements around the room. Besides natural light that comes through kitchen windows in the daytime, there are three basic types of light you can use to enhance your kitchen: general, task, and accent.

Natural light. The more natural light you can get into a kitchen, the more open and spacious it will feel (top). Consider giving up a bit of wall space for larger windows. Alternatively, think about skylights; they can bring in light without sacrificing storage space.

Accent lighting. Decorative or accent lighting is designed to show off your kitchen (middle). Whether it's something as simple as enhancing a cabinet with interior lighting (as shown here) or adding a wall sconce or even light strips above the cabinets, you can create a completely different look or mood simply by flipping a switch.

Task lighting. Task lighting (like the under-cabinet light shown at far right) puts light where you need it to perform tasks such as food preparation. Recessed lights mounted over a range or sink are another example. Under-cabinet lights are typically either strip or single "puck" halogen lights. They're usually low-voltage and can be installed with ease (see page 173).

General lighting. General lighting (bottom) lets you move around the kitchen safely, see inside cabinets and drawers, and perform basic kitchen tasks. In days past, general lighting consisted of an incandescent or fluorescent overhead. Today, the trend is toward recessed lighting. Pendant lights like the ones shown here are extremely popular over islands and peninsulas.

Photo courtesy of Hy-Lite Products, Inc.

Photo courtesy of LG Hi-Macs

HARDWARE

Photos courtesy of Amerock

■ The hardware you choose for your cabinets can make or break the overall look of the kitchen. This may sound a bit strong, but it's true. Cabinet hardware can be bland, it can blend in with the cabinets, it can serve as a transition between materials (such as stainless steel pulls on dark maple cabinets with a stainless steel countertop), or it can create a bold statement.

Gone are the days when you chose between a ceramic knob (white) or pulls in silver, gold, brass, or copper finish in one of three or four styles. Now, the choices are staggering. You'll find all types of materials: plastic, ceramic, metal, glass—even stone. Finishes vary as well: sand-blasted, highly textured, ultra-smooth...you name it.

Styles range from classic round knobs to handmade metal creations. Pulls in particular have enjoyed a renaissance in style: fun shapes such as knives, forks, and spoons, wavy lines, fruits and vegetables, bugs, flowers, and animals, to name a few.

If you can't decide between a couple of choices, buy one or two of each and take them home. Remove your existing hardware and attach the new ones, take a step back, and compare. If the hole spacing doesn't allow this, attach the new knobs or pulls to the cabinet with a piece of reusable adhesive putty. Note: If the pull holes don't match up and you're planning on painting the cabinets (see pages 82–83), you may want to consider another choice because you'll have to fill the old holes and drill new holes for the new hardware.

COLOR

Photo courtesy of General Electric

■ Years ago, when you wanted to add color in the kitchen, your options were limited to painting or wallpapering walls, and maybe buying an appliance in avocado or harvest gold. Now, though, you can find cabinets, fixtures, and appliances in a wide (and sometimes wild) assortment of colors.

Walls. Changing the walls of the kitchen is still one of the best ways to add color (top). Paint, wallpaper, and even tile are inexpensive and allow you to easily alter the look when it's time for a change.

Cabinets. Many manufacturers are adding bold color choices to their cabinet selection (right). Be careful here, though: What might seem like a great color today could get old in a year or two. And, replacing the cabinets is an expensive proposition. Make sure the cabinets you buy can be repainted if desired.

Photo courtesy of Heartland Appliances

Fixtures. Kitchen plumbing fixtures, both sinks and faucets, are now available in a rainbow of colors (middle). Since either of these is simple to replace and relatively inexpensive, this is a good way to highlight an accent color in the kitchen.

Photo courtesy of Moen

Photo courtesy of Heartland Appliances

Appliances. Appliance colors range from bold tones (like the stove shown at bottom right) to muted pastels (like the '50s refrigerator at near right). As with cabinets, take care in choosing a color you'll be happy with for a while, as these will be expensive to replace. It's a shame to have to buy a replacement appliance when there's nothing wrong with the old one except for the color.

Photo courtesy of Elmira Stove Works

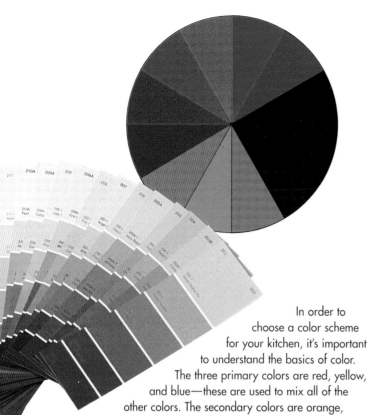

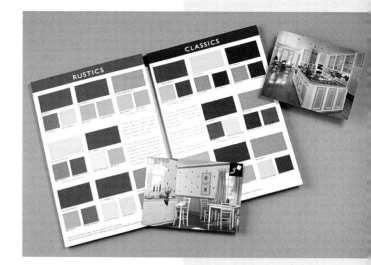

In order to choose a color scheme for your kitchen, it's important to understand the basics of color. The three primary colors are red, yellow, and blue—these are used to mix all of the other colors. The secondary colors are orange, green, and violet—they are each mixed from equal parts of two primaries. In between these come a vast number of intermediate colors; see the color wheel above. To pick a contrast color (say, for an accent), choose a color that's opposite it on the color wheel. For example, a contrast to blue is orange. When looking for colors that will blend well, choose adjacent colors (such as yellow-green and green). When you mix white with one of these pure colors, you get a pastel.

You should also know that colors look different in different types of light: Incandescents emphasize reds and yellows, fluorescents highlight blues. That's why you should bring paint chips and wallpaper samples home and see how they look in your kitchen before deciding on a color; never choose these at the home center. Also, the amount of color you use affects how you'll see it. A bright red may make an excellent backsplash accent, but may be too much for an entire wall. And finally, every color affects the colors around it; make sure to hold chips and samples next to each other in the kitchen when choosing.

When it's time to choose a color theme, there are three basic ones to choose from: monochromatic, analogous, and complementary. A monochromatic scheme uses shades, tints, and intensities of a single color. An analogous theme combines variations of colors that are close to each other on the color wheel, such as yellow, yellow-orange, and orange. A complementary theme uses combinations of complementary (contrasting) colors such as red and green, or violet and yellow.

Since colors create moods, it's often best to start by picking the primary "mood" color you want. Reds, pinks, oranges, and yellows are warm; soft greens and blues are cool and peaceful; and contrasting colors are bright and bold. Choosing colors can be confusing, and paint companies try to make it easier by providing color palettes to choose from. Color cards like the ones above left are a great starting point.

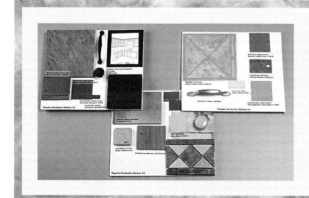

COLOR BOARDS

■ Many kitchen designers create color boards like the ones shown here to help customers envision what their new kitchen will look like. You can do the same for your makeover. Attach samples to a piece of foam board with glue: flooring, tile, paint chips, and hardware. Bringing all the parts together like this can be a real eye-opener… and may prompt you to make some major changes ahead of time.

CHOOSING MATERIALS

In kitchens, like everything else, you get what you pay for…usually. You don't always have to pay high-end prices to get high-end look and performance, as long as you're making informed choices.

For example, granite and quartz countertops are trendy now, but a laminate lookalike can cost a fraction of the price. Or maybe you crave that famous-name, stainless-steel refrigerator—you can have the same look from an everyday brand for a lot less.

Whether it's cabinets or cars, differences in construction and materials may or may not be worth the sticker prices. When you know something about the product before walking into the cabinet aisle, you'll be able to sift through the sales chat, and make a more confident choice. Without question, the selections in materials, colors, and price levels in today's market can be overwhelming… if you don't know what to look for. So get a little smarter about choosing materials, and you can be much more money-smart about your kitchen project.

FLOORING

■ Where's the Grand Central Station in your home? The kitchen. With all the traffic it gets, the kitchen flooring you choose needs to be durable, moisture-resistant, easy to clean—and finally, attractive. Although many folks tend to select flooring by appearance, it's best to look at durability first, then choose a color and pattern that complement your kitchen design.

There are four main types of flooring that work well in a kitchen: sheet vinyl, vinyl tiles, ceramic tiles, and laminate flooring. In addition to withstanding a lot of traffic, the floor in a kitchen has to be able to handle food and water spills. Water is the biggest danger. The flooring must be able to prevent the water from penetrating into the flooring itself, and, just as important, keep the water away from the subfloor, which may be highly susceptible to water damage. This is particularly true if your subfloor is particleboard; particleboard will soak up water and expand like a sponge.

You'll notice that solid-wood flooring isn't on the list of recommended flooring types. That's because if there is a leak, or a large water spill (an overflowing sink, perhaps), the flooring will soak up the water—even when sealed with a clear finish. Regardless of the type of wood flooring (tongue-and-groove strips or planks, or parquet tiles), the wood would warp and twist. And repairing a damaged floor like this is a real headache in terms of inconvenience, repair time, and cost. If you want the look of wood, consider a laminate flooring (see the opposite page).

Sheet vinyl: Sheet vinyl remains the most popular material choice for both new kitchens and makeovers. There are many good reasons for this: It's inexpensive, comfortable to walk on, stain-resistant, and easy to care for, and it comes in a dizzying array of colors, patterns, and textures. Sheet vinyl comes in standard 12-foot rolls and is cut to length as needed. It does take care and patience to install, but if you can install it with no seams, it's virtually impervious to water. On the downside, vinyl flooring dents fairly easily (especially the economy grades) and must be installed on a very flat and smooth subfloor.

Vinyl tiles. Vinyl tiles are typically 12" squares; they can be backed with an adhesive that makes installation a breeze—just peel and stick. Or they can be plain-backed, and attached to the floor with adhesive. Although messier than peel-and-stick, glued-on tiles tend to hold up better over time. As with sheet vinyl, vinyl tiles must be installed on a super-flat and smooth surface. The disadvantage to vinyl tiles is there are many more seams for water and dirt to sneak through and loosen the adhesive.

Ceramic tile. Just like tile countertops, tiled floors are relatively do-it-yourself friendly because it's easy to re-cut a tile if you make a mistake. Choose a floor tile that has a matte or textured finish, and avoid glossy tiles; they're slippery underfoot. There are a few disadvantages to tile floors. First, they don't offer any "give" and so can be hard on the feet. Second, the hard tile is cold, "noisy," and unforgiving if you drop a dish or glass.

Photo courtesy of Wellborn Cabinet

Laminate. Laminate flooring is often called a "floating" floor because it doesn't attach directly to the subfloor. Instead, it rests on a thin cushion and is held down by the baseboard around the perimeter of the room. The material is similar to plastic laminate and features a decorative paper that's bonded to high-density fiberboard and covered with melamine plastic. Color and pattern choices range from wood-like flooring to faux ceramic tile. Laminate flooring is easy to install: The planks are interlocking and are simply glued together. This material is relatively expensive, but extremely durable as long as it's sealed properly (see page 78 for more on this).

CABINETS

■ If you're planning to replace some or all of the cabinets in your kitchen, you'll need to know a bit about how they're made and what they're made of, to make an intelligent purchase decision. Although you'll likely be tempted to start shopping for style first, it's best to define what type of cabinets you're after and use this to narrow the choices for style. It's easy to fall in love with the "perfect" cabinet style, only to find out it's low-quality and won't meet all your needs.

Construction types. There are three basic types of construction used to build the cabinets that you'll find in most kitchens: site-built, framed, and frameless.

Site-built cabinets. You'll find site-built cabinets in many older homes (right). As the name implies, these were actually constructed on site. The carpenter may have cut parts to size in the shop, but the cabinets were assembled in the kitchen. You can usually identify a site-built cabinet by looking closely at the dividers between the cabinets and at the backs of the cabinets. If there is no back and the dividers are a single thickness of plywood or particleboard, the cabinet was built on site.

Instead of attaching separate modular cabinets together, site-built cabinets are assembled using common parts: The bottom of the cabinet is typically one piece, as are the braces attached to the backs of the dividers. The dividers are shared from one compartment to the next. A single face frame was usually assembled and then attached to the front of the cabinet in one piece. And the countertop, typically plywood, was one piece and was fastened to the cabinet. Then plastic laminate was glued to this.

Photo courtesy of American Woodmark

Although this method of construction did save on materials, site-built cabinets are a pain to work on. Say, for example, you want to replace just the countertop. You can't simply pry it off, because you'll risk damaging the cabinets—especially if the plywood was secured with screws. Also, to remove the cabinets, you basically have to disassemble them in the reverse order they were constructed. Any of these tasks requires patience along with a knowledge of how they were made.

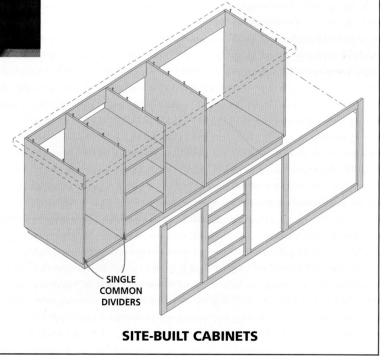

SINGLE COMMON DIVIDERS

SITE-BUILT CABINETS

Face-frame cabinets. As manufacturing processes evolved, so did the kitchen cabinet industry. They quickly realized that it would be faster for an installer to assemble pre-made cabinets than to build custom cabinets to fit. The standard cabinet they developed is still widely used today: the face-frame cabinet.

The sides, back, top, and bottom are made of thin material joined together with glue and staples. The cabinet strength comes from a solid wood frame that's attached to the front of the cabinet. Doors and drawers are then cut to fit the openings. Because the face frame reduces the size of the openings, there is less interior storage space—especially for drawers. On the plus side, face-frame cabinets are the easiest to install because any gaps can be filled with filler strips (see page 102 for more on these).

The face frames are typically $1^1/4$"- to $1^1/2$"-wide, $3/4$"-thick hardwood. On quality cabinets the frame parts are joined with mortises and tenons, or at the very least dowels. The sides and bottom can range anywhere from $1/4$" to $3/4$" particleboard or plywood. Three-quarter-inch-thick plywood is the sturdiest. Back panels are usually $1/8$"-thick hardboard. The back and bottom typically fit in dadoes or grooves in the sides. Corner brackets help hold the parts together and also provide a means for securing the countertop.

FACE FRAME

FACE-FRAME CABINET

CABINETS, *continued*

Frameless cabinets. The final construction method, frameless cabinets, has been popular in Europe for many years. This method uses fewer materials than face-frame cabinets and offers a clean, contemporary look. Frameless cabinets are often referred to as 32mm cabinets because this is the increment which all holes, hinge fittings, cabinet joints, and mountings are set apart. Since this construction method originated in Europe, the metric system was used throughout.

The sides, top, and bottom are typically manufactured from $3/4$"-thick particleboard. Because of this added thickness, the cabinet parts when assembled are sufficiently strong and do not need a face frame to provide support. This opens up the full interior space for storage. Full-overlay doors are mounted via fully adjustable hinges that attach to the inside of the cabinet.

Since the cabinets don't have face frames, extreme care must be taken in ordering and installing these, as any filler strip used will be painfully obvious. Also, there are some concerns about the stability of the cabinets over time: They can exhibit a tendency to "rack" or twist out of shape and alignment, since there's no face frame to prevent this from occurring. When it's time to order your new cabinets, you'll find three basic types to choose from: stock, semi-custom, and custom. Stock cabinets are constructed either in advance or on an on-demand basis. Most stock

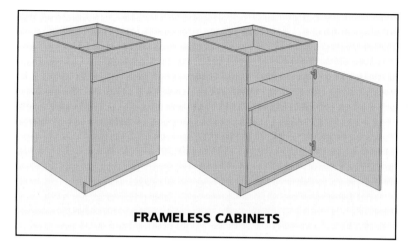

FRAMELESS CABINETS

UNDERSTANDING CABINET CODE

■ If you need to order or purchase your own cabinets—or you're working with a designer—you'll encounter a code that's used almost universally to describe cabinets. The code consists of a combination of letters and numbers (up to 11) as follows:

The first letter defines the category: W = wall, T = tall, B = base, V = vanity, D = desk, and F = furniture.

The second set of characters identifies the cabinet type. Here are some examples: BB = blind base corner cabinet, BC = base corner cabinet, BD = base cabinet with drawers.

The next two numbers define the width of the cabinet. Most manufacturers make cabinets in 3" increments, ranging from 9" to 48".

The cabinet height is noted with the next numbers. These are used only if there are varying heights to choose from. Since base cabinets are a standard height ($34^{1}/_{2}$"), this is used only for wall cabinets.

The final two characters describe any non-standard features, such as GD = glass doors and TO = tilt-out drawer.

So, a DB24 is a 24"-wide base unit with drawers, and a WC2430D is a 30" high, diagonal 45-degree corner unit with a single door. Simple, right? Fortunately, most cabinet catalogs have line drawings of each cabinet so you can locate it by appearance and then specify the code number.

cabinet manufacturers offer a wide array of sizes and styles. These are the least expensive of the cabinets, and delivery is usually quick because the odds are good they've got the standard sizes in stock. The disadvantage to these is that you're limited to the sizes they offer. If you need a cabinet custom-made, you'll have to go to a cabinet shop or to another manufacturer.

Semi-custom cabinets are the next step up from stock cabinets. Semi-custom manufacturers do make some stock cabinets, but they make most on an on-demand basis. You'll find a wider choice of cabinet sizes and styles, along with greater offerings in terms of accessories such as interior fittings. Some true custom sizes and fittings are possible, but at a substantial cost.

Custom cabinets are all made to order. Although custom cabinet manufacturers tend to stick with the 3" units, fully custom sizes are possible. Since these are all custom-made, there is no warehouse full of stock cabinets.

Photo courtesy of Timberlake Cabinet Company

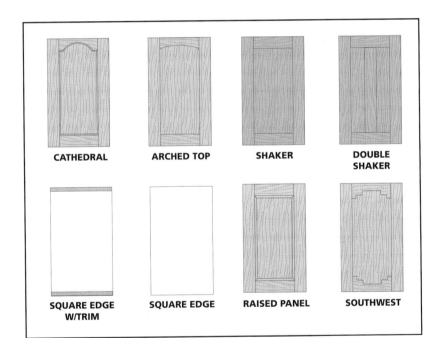

CATHEDRAL **ARCHED TOP** **SHAKER** **DOUBLE SHAKER**

SQUARE EDGE W/TRIM **SQUARE EDGE** **RAISED PANEL** **SOUTHWEST**

This usually means a significant wait between the order and delivery. But custom cabinet makers usually offer the latest and greatest accessories, as well as superior materials and construction methods. Drawers are assembled with dovetails, and doors have solid mortise-and-tenon construction. Custom finishes are also possible—all it takes is money.

DOOR AND DRAWER STYLES

■ Regardless of the construction method you choose, the overall appearance of the cabinet will depend primarily on the door and drawer style. Your choices range from a simple full-overlay door to highly sculpted doors, such as the raised-panel cathedral door shown at left. Note that most designers will specify the more ornate doors (like cathedral) for wall cabinets only; since base cabinets are less visible, they're typically fitted with plain doors in the same style. Common woods for doors and drawer fronts include oak, maple, cherry, hickory, and pecan. Tight-grained woods such as maple and cherry tend to resist stains better than open-grained woods like oak.

COUNTERTOPS

■ Of all the choices you make regarding the kitchen, the material you select for the countertop must be the hardest-working. No other surface, not even the floor, will get the constant abuse a countertop gets: hot pots and pans, liquid spills, vigorous scrubbing and cleaning, abrasion from everything from kids' backpacks to daily dishes.

Although plastic laminate has been the prevailing countertop of choice for many years (and it's still a good choice), it's steadily being replaced by solid-surface countertops such as Corian and Zodiaq. Because these countertops are solid all the way through, the edges can be milled to any profile, the top can be routed for drainage, and recesses can be made to accept decorative inlays for a truly unique look. Here are the pros and cons of some of the most popular countertop choices.

Stone: With their highly buffed surfaces and natural beauty, marble and granite countertops are becoming increasing popular in modern kitchens. The cool surfaces of both these materials are excellent for working with dough or making candy. But with their extremely high cost and their tendency to stain, you may want to use them sparingly in a kitchen—such as in a small slab for a baking center. Because these materials are quite heavy, they need a stout base and should always be installed professionally.

Photo courtesy of DuPont Corian

COMPARING COUNTERTOP MATERIALS

Material	Cost	Installation	Advantage	Disadvantage
Plastic laminate	$	Easy, especially if custom-ordered	Inexpensive, yet durable	Limited edge treatments
Solid-surface	$$$	Certified fabricator only	No visible seams; edges and surface can be shaped and inlaid; surface can be renewed	Scratches easier than stone and quartz; can be discolored by heat
Tile	$	Easy, but messy and time-consuming	Inexpensive and lends itself to custom shapes	Grout lines can stain
Quartz	$$$$	Certified fabricator only	Excellent depth and clarity; strong; doesn't stain	Seams are visible
Stone	$$$$	Professional, but homeowner can install if custom cut	Beautiful natural patterns; strong; does not promote bacteria growth	Seams are visible
Concrete	$$$	Professional only	Impervious to most stains; no seams	Long installation time; cabinets need to be reinforced to handle the extra weight

Concrete: At first blush, using concrete for a countertop might seem crazy. But you'd be surprised what some creative concrete folks are doing with this hardy material. Unlike its high-gloss cousins, a concrete surface offers a rustic, textured appeal. Like natural stone, a concrete countertop is heavy and requires a sturdy base. It's also fairly absorbent and must be sealed to prevent staining. This is not a do-it-yourself project. Because of the time-consuming hand work involved, concrete countertops are expensive.

Plastic laminate. This super-tough material (top) is made of several layers of resin-impregnated paper bonded to a colorful top layer of paper and then covered with clear melamine plastic. This is then bonded to a particleboard core that may or may not have a backsplash. Plastic laminate's well-deserved reputation for durability combined with low cost and easy cleanup make this an excellent choice for makeovers on a tight budget.

Solid-surface materials. Solid-surface material (such as Corian) is made from acrylic resins and mineral fillers that are formed into $1/2$"-thick sheets for countertops (left). You can even get sinks made out of this stuff—when the sink is bonded to the countertop, no seams will show. Solid-surface countertops are easy to clean and water-resistant, and unlike thin laminate, you can sand out blemishes in this thicker top. On the downside, this material does stain more readily than plastic laminate, it's expensive, and it usually requires professional installation.

Quartz. For the ultimate in solid-surface countertops, consider quartz (like the Zodiaq quartz shown at left). It's composed mostly of quartz (93%), which makes it exceptionally tough. A quartz countertop is dense and nonporous, and no sealing is required. In addition to being strong and durable, quartz is heat-, scratch-, and stain-resistant. It's easy to maintain and offers unusual depth, clarity, and radiance. And it does not promote the growth of mold, mildew, or bacteria.

Ceramic tile: Ceramic tile (bottom) is one of the most do-it-yourself-friendly materials for countertops. Individual tiles are more forgiving than a large sheet of plastic laminate or natural stone. If you mess up a tile, just cut another. Ceramic tiles are inexpensive and are available in a huge assortment of colors, shapes, sizes, and textures. When installed correctly, they're heat-proof, scratch- and water-resistant, and long-lasting. The disadvantage to a ceramic tile countertop is the grout: It stains easily and is difficult to keep clean. You can minimize this by using thin grout lines and by sealing the grout frequently. Colored grout? It's another option, but it just hides some stains better—it won't prevent them.

SINKS

Photo courtesy of Kohler

Photo courtesy of Moen

■ Your kitchen sink is the most-used plumbing fixture in your house. So, choosing one that will serve you well and provide the look and feel you're after takes some thought. Shopping for a kitchen sink isn't like it was when our grandparents first bought one; they had a choice between white or white, and maybe one or two styles. Today, of course, we have have many more choices. In order of importance, you'll need to choose how the sink is mounted, what it's made from, the number and size of bowls—and of course, the color and style.

Kitchen sinks are often classified by how they are mounted: true self-rimming, self-rimming with clips, flush with tile, under-counter, and seamless (see the sidebar below). Once you've decided on the mounting style, it's time to select the material. The most common choices here are stainless steel, porcelain over cast iron, and composite or solid surface (see the opposite page).

Number of and size of bowls. How many bowls, and their sizes, is your next decision. Bowls vary from one to three, and they can be identical in size and depth, or vary. Deeper-bowled sinks are becoming more popular, as well as sinks with a smaller bowl inset between two larger bowls. The smaller middle bowl frequently has a garbage disposal attached to it. Bowl number and size is really a matter of personal preference. If you pick a larger sink, just make sure that it fits in your countertop.

SINK MOUNTING OPTIONS

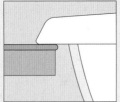 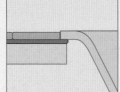 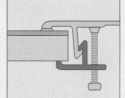 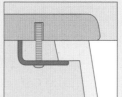 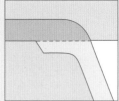

True self-rimming cast iron or porcelain sinks are held in place by their significant weight and a thin layer of sealant or plumber's putty that forms a watertight seal under the small flat section on the rim.

Although called self-rimming, this style of sink really isn't. To create a watertight seal, a dozen or so small clips hook onto a lip on the underside of the sink and pull the sink down tight.

Installing a sink so that it ends up flush with the countertop can be achieved by first installing the sink and then building up the countertop around it, such as when tiling.

Under-counter sinks have become popular with the advent of solid-surface materials. This style of sink presses up under the counter and is held in place with clips that screw into embedded inserts.

The ultimate solution to stopping water from leaking between a sink and its countertop is to form the sink and countertop as one unit, out of the same material, and glue them together.

Stainless steel. For a long time, stainless steel sinks were seen as the ultimate kitchen sink material. Virtually free from staining, this hardy metal could even be buffed out when scratched. And stainless steel is still an excellent option; relatively inexpensive, it's easy to find and to install. Its one disadvantage, being loud, has been overcome by many sink makers who've attached dampening strips to the bowls to deaden sound.

Photo courtesy of Sterling

Photo courtesy of Kohler

Photo courtesy of Moen

Cast iron. There's just something satisfying about using a cast-iron sink. Maybe it's that it's so quiet. Or that it is massive and unmoving. The combination of the tough porcelain coating along with the heavy cast iron makes a formidable unit. Unfortunately, what makes it so nice to use is also a problem. Cast-iron sinks are not flexible. If you drop a dish in one, the dish will probably break. This isn't true of many of the other, more flexible materials. And the porcelain surface, although hard, can be chipped easily if a metal knife or pot is dropped in the sink.

Composite. A relative newcomer to the sink market, composite sinks offer a huge advantage over other sink materials—that is, if they're being installed into a similar material countertop. Their advantage is they can be glued to the underside of the countertop with special adhesives that will create a virtually seamless bond. Not only does this eliminate the possibility of leaks, it also creates smooth-flowing lines and a rimless sink. There's no edge to capture food particles; no edge to interfere with wiping off the countertop. The only disadvantage to these currently is the choice of available features: bowl shape and size, along with color (typically white), are quite limited. That's not to say that you can't get a custom composite sink (like the one shown here), as long as you're willing to spend quite a bit more.

Photo courtesy of Kohler

FAUCETS

■ It's time for a new faucet. So you go to the local home center and find a virtual wall of faucets to choose from. Buy a name you can trust and don't skimp on cost. A quality faucet will provide years of trouble-free service. But which one on the wall is for you? Odds are you've got an idea of the style you're after, but what about the finish? Spout type? Type of control? And what kind of sprayer, if any?

Finish. It used to be that all kitchen faucets had a chrome finish. Chrome held up well, was easy to clean, and looked good. And chrome is still a good choice. You'll also find high-gloss brass or gold finishes as well as a number of brushed finishes like brushed stainless steel, copper, pewter, and nickel. The advantage of any brushed finish is that it doesn't show fingerprints like a high-gloss finish does. There are also plastic or enamel finishes available in a rainbow of colors. Be aware that these can chip much like a porcelain sink, leaving the underlying metal bare.

Photo courtesy of Danze

Photo courtesy of Moen

Photo courtesy of Moen

Spout type. Kitchen faucet spouts have steadily evolved from the standard angled pivot spout common to most homes. New shapes (such as the gooseneck shown above center) make it easier to fill tall containers as well as having a graceful appearance. Other versions tackle the same problem by allowing you to pull up the spout (above). Probably the most popular solution is the pull-out sprayer (see the sidebar at right).

Control type. Finally, you'll need to decide whether you want separate controls or a single control. This is entirely a matter of personal preference. Just keep in mind that the fewer the controls, the more holes you'll have available on the sink for other accessories such as a soap or hot water dispenser.

SPRAYER OPTIONS

Side mount. The classic sprayer configuration has it mounted in a separate hole to the side of the faucet; this requires a four-holed sink.

Baseplate mount. Some newer faucets offer a baseplate-mounted sprayer so you can use the fourth sink hole for a soap or hot water dispenser.

Pull-out. An even niftier version is a sprayer that pulls out of the faucet and then slips back in for normal use.

Photos courtesy of Moen

WALLS

■ Since most of the wall space in your kitchen will be taken up by cabinets, the areas that do show provide an opportunity to add color and texture. Wall covering options include paint, wallpaper, tile or stone, and even wood, such as wainscoting.

Paint. Paint is by far the simplest wall covering in the kitchen. Its biggest advantage is it's so easy to change if you want a new look—just brush on a new coat. To make cleanup easier, choose a satin- or eggshell-finish latex paint. Avoid flat paints, as they are tougher to keep clean. Some specialty paints provide texture such as suede, and faux finishes like ragging can create the look of texture.

Wallpaper. Vinyl wallpaper is an excellent choice for the kitchen since it's fairly impervious to stains. It comes in a wide array of patterns and colors, but it does take more time to apply than paint. Some wallpapers also offer textures that simulate surfaces such as bamboo or woven cloth. When shopping for wallpaper, choose the strippable variety; you'll appreciate this feature when it comes time to remove it for a new look.

Tile or stone. Ceramic tile is one of the best wall coverings for the backsplash area. It's stain-resistant and easy to clean and install. Four-inch tiles and smaller mosaic tiles work best for this, and they also come in many colors, patterns, and textures. An inexpensive way to add a nice accent is to install a handmade or sculpted tile at regular intervals. These specialty tiles can be quite expensive but are affordable in small quantities. Stone veneer makes a bold statement for a backsplash or wall section but is best installed professionally.

APPLIANCES

■ If new appliances are part of your makeover, take the time up front to select them—especially if new cabinets are being installed. There's not a cabinet designer out there who will start a job until you've first selected the appliances. That's because the cabinets are then designed to fit around them. If you did it the other way 'round, you'd be faced with selecting appliances by size, and odds are you won't end up with the features you want. Unfortunately, this is often what happens with a makeover where the cabinets are unchanged, except maybe for appearance (painting, refacing, etc.). If this is the case for you, carefully measure each existing appliance opening and use these measurements to narrow down your choices.

Refrigerators. Years ago, most refrigerators were a standard size. But homeowners have asked for increasingly larger food storage space, as well as extra features such as exterior water and ice dispensers. Manufacturers have responded by making larger and larger units. Regardless of the door configuration (side by side or top and bottom), note that in addition to being wider and taller, many larger units are deeper, too. Unless the refrigerator is installed into a built-in alcove, the extra depth will make the refrigerator stick out considerably past any adjacent countertops. In response to this, some makers are building counter-depth units. Another way to mask this extra depth is to install a built-in refrigerator, where the cabinetry is brought out flush with the doors of the unit.

Photo courtesy of General Electric

Dishwashers. The dishwasher is one of the few appliances that actually is fairly standard in dimensions. Most will fit in a 24"-wide space under a countertop. The reason they're confined to these dimensions is so they'll fit into a standard base cabinet. If the manufacturers were to alter the size, you'd have to get custom base cabinets made to fit. Besides selecting a finish for the front door (white, bone, black, stainless steel, etc.), you'll have to choose a capacity and the features. Both of these depend on how you intend to use the dishwasher. The biggest complaint you'll hear about dishwashers is how loud they are. Some manufacturers (like Bosch; model shown here) have engineered units that are surprisingly quiet.

Ranges. The big decision when selecting a range is, which type of heat: gas or electric? Sometimes this decision is made for you if you don't have a gas line (as in many rural areas). Professional chefs find gas best for cooking. A gas cooktop heats up instantly, offers precise heat control, and cools off quickly. But what chefs don't mention is that their cooktops are professional-grade—that is, capable of generating more heat (15,000 BTUs versus 9,000 to 12,000 for standard residential units). Professionals need higher heat quickly both to fill orders and to use certain cooking techniques. (That's why a steak at a restaurant tastes better than at home—it's seared faster with higher heat to seal in the flavor.)

There are a couple of things to keep in mind if you decide to step up to a professional-grade range or cooktop. First, these units are often very heavy; you may need to reinforce the floor beneath. Second, because of the higher heat these ranges generate, the wall behind the unit and any nearby cabinets must be covered with a heat-resistant material such as cement board. And finally, higher heats demand large ventilation systems to remove the excess heat.

Photo courtesy of Viking

Gas range. Gas is considered by far the best heat for ranges, as it offers instant heat and quick cooking times. Gas units also cool down quickly when turned off but can be a challenge to clean.

Photo courtesy of Gaggenau

Separate cooktop. Another cooking option that has become increasingly popular is a separate cooktop. Behind its popularity? The wall oven (see page 38). As soon as the oven was separated from the cooktop, it opened up a number of possibilities that didn't exist before. That's because a cooktop is only a few inches deep. This means you can install one almost anywhere—in islands, peninsulas, etc. And because a cooktop fits in an opening cut into a countertop, it offers a custom built-in appearance that you don't get even from a built-in range.

Electric range.
A step up from the outdated coil-type electric cooktop (right), modern ranges heat up quickly but cool down slower. Halogen units are capable of almost instant heat, but at a much higher cost. The ceramic tops, or smooth-tops, also make cleanup a snap.

Photo courtesy of KitchenAid

Dual-fuel range. If you want the best of both heating worlds, consider a dual-fuel range like the one shown here. These typically use gas for the cooktop and electricity to heat the oven.

Wall ovens. Whoever came up with the idea of a wall oven deserves a medal. Anyone who has ever struggled, bent over, trying to lift a Thanksgiving turkey out of a standard range oven will appreciate a wall oven—at least, their back will. Wall ovens

Photo courtesy of Gaggenau

are installed up at a comfortable working height. Not only does this make it much easier to use, but it also lets you keep an eye on the food without bending over. Wall ovens are available in single or double units; some come with warming trays as well. Heat may be gas or electric, with electric becoming more popular with the advent of the convection oven. In a convection oven, an element heats the air and a fan circulates it to provide more even cooking, often with shorter times.

COOKTOP VENTING OPTIONS

Photo courtesy of Gaggenau

Photo courtesy of Viking

Downdraft. On a downdraft range or cooktop, either a built-in or a remote blower pulls moisture, odor, and contaminants down into the unit, pushes them through a filter, and then exhausts them outdoors. Types include pop-up (as shown here, left) and surface-mount.

Photo courtesy of Gaggenau

Photo courtesy of Faber

Range hood. A separate range hood can be wall- or ceiling-mounted above the cooktop. These units (especially large ones) do a terrific job of clearing the air in a kitchen. Because they are so large, they often become the focal point—whether you want them to be or not.

Photo courtesy of General Electric

Under-cabinet. Under-cabinet ventilation units are often combined with a microwave to conserve counter space. These units draw moisture, odors, and contaminants up through a filter and either exhaust this outdoors or recirculate it back into the kitchen.

LIGHTING

■ The kitchen is one of the most complicated rooms in your home to light. That's because you need so many types of lighting: general, task, and accent.

Fortunately, there is a huge variety of lights to choose from; so many, in fact, that choosing is often the hardest part of the job (see the illustration at right).

In older kitchens, all the lighting typically came from a single overhead fixture, either incandescent or fluorescent. Modern kitchens usually use a combination of natural light from windows and recessed cans in the ceiling. Task lighting—lighting designed to illuminate a specific area, such as a countertop used for food preparation—is usually under-cabinet lights in the form of strips or "pucks." Accent lighting can be anything from interior cabinet lights to pendants to wall sconces.

When selecting recessed cans, make sure to choose the type that's rated for insulation contact. These lights can be installed in the ceiling without having to move the insulation out of the way (which will create an unwanted path for warm air to leak out of your kitchen). For the ultimate in flexibility, choose cans that have pivoting lenses so you can direct the light where you need it most. When choosing under-cabinet lighting, go with halogen—it creates a light more natural than fluorescents, which tend to cast a greenish tint on surfaces.

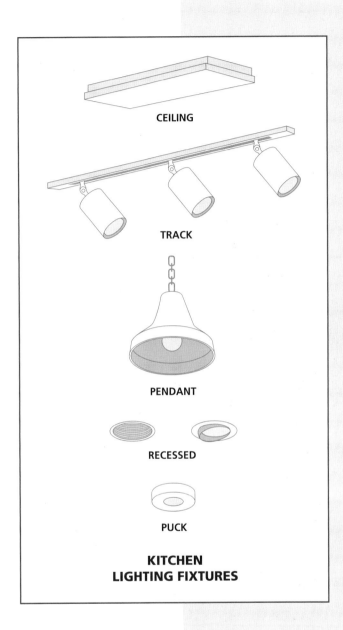

CEILING

TRACK

PENDANT

RECESSED

PUCK

**KITCHEN
LIGHTING FIXTURES**

KITCHEN SYSTEMS

This chapter heading may not be glamorous, but boy, is it essential. Say you want to install a dishwasher where none exists now. You just cut out a cabinet or two, pop in the unit, and push a button, right? How about the electricity and the plumbing? Is there a waste line to tap into, and sufficient electrical service? The point is, the "mundane" aspects of a kitchen can make or break your plans.

The systems help make the kitchen the most complicated room in the house. You have electrical, including ground-fault receptacles: 110-volt and 220-volt plus lighting; plumbing, including supply and waste lines to one sink (if not two), and separate lines for dishwashers and ice makers; ventilation that removes grease- and odor-laden air from the kitchen. Plus, the kitchen has the same heating and cooling requirements as every other room in the home.

From ice makers to cooktops, the placement and use of many standard kitchen items are dictated by how your particular systems are set up. Here are the basics you need to know.

PLUMBING SYSTEM

■ The plumbing system in your kitchen consists of three types of lines: supply, waste, and vent. How complex these are depends on how many fixtures and appliances there are. The average kitchen has a single sink, a dishwasher, and an ice maker hookup (see the illustration below).

Supply lines. The supply system directs pressurized water to the plumbing fixtures. Fresh water enters the home via a local water utility or from a private well; the pressure comes from the city's pumping stations or from the well pump, respectively. Regardless of the source, the water flows through a main shutoff valve (and a water meter if supplied by a utility), and then to the hot water heater. From there, both hot and cold water branch out to various parts of the home. All lines terminate in some sort of valve that, when opened, will allow water to flow. Valves such as sink faucets are operated manually; other valves like those in refrigerator ice makers are automatic.

Waste line. The waste line transports solid and liquid waste out of the home. It relies on gravity to move the wastewater from sinks and dishwashers away from the fixture and into a line (often called the soil stack) that empties into the municipal sewer or a private septic tank. In between every fixture and the waste line is a trap—basically a curved section of pipe that captures or "traps" water. The trap fills with sufficient water to form an airtight seal to prevent sewer gas from entering the home.

Vent line. The vent line does two important jobs. First, it allows the wastewater in the drain line to flow freely. Second, it prevents siphoning, which can pull the water out of traps, allowing sewer gas into the home. In both cases, a vent line does its job by

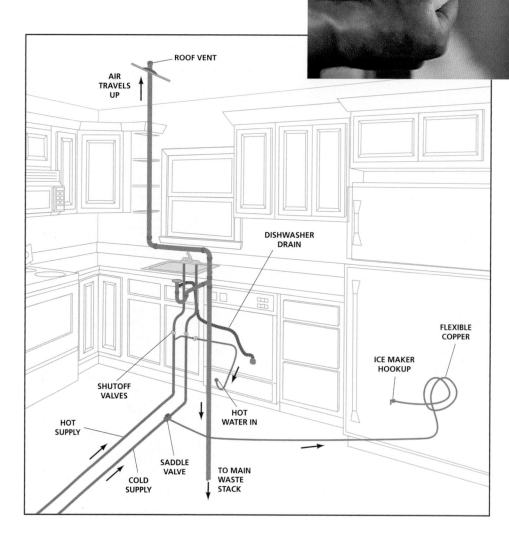

ROOF VENT

AIR TRAVELS UP

DISHWASHER DRAIN

FLEXIBLE COPPER

ICE MAKER HOOKUP

SHUTOFF VALVES

HOT WATER IN

HOT SUPPLY

SADDLE VALVE

COLD SUPPLY

TO MAIN WASTE STACK

allowing fresh air to flow into the drain line the same way the second hole (or vent) in a gas can allows the gas to flow out freely. Vents are connected along each fixture's drain line past the trap. In addition to allowing fresh air in, vents also allow sewer gas to flow out of the home and harmlessly up through a roof vent.

Plumbing code. You'll need a permit anytime you consider adding to or changing existing plumbing, running new plumbing, or upgrading substandard plumbing. Although this may seem a nuisance, plumbing codes are written and enforced to protect you. Part of the confusion associated with plumbing codes is that what is perfectly acceptable in one part of the country may be prohibited in another part. It's important to note that your local plumbing code supersedes the national code that it amends. The only way to make sure is to check the code at your local building department.

KITCHEN SINK VENT LINE

■ Since most kitchens have windows directly above the sink, you need to know that the vent line will typically run up and around the window as shown here. This is important if you're planning on moving or enlarging the window—the vent line may need to be re-routed, and you should consider the cost of this in your makeover budget.

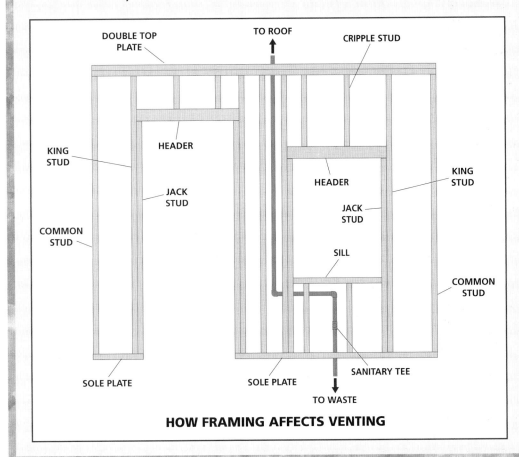

HOW FRAMING AFFECTS VENTING

ELECTRICAL SYSTEM

■ The kitchen is one of the most complicated electrical rooms in the home, as it typically requires both 110-volt and 220-volt circuits, many of which are dedicated to a single appliance. Electricity from the local utility company connects to your home through the service head. It flows through the electric company's meter and then enters the house at the service panel. Here it is distributed throughout the house and to the kitchen via individual circuits, each protected by either a fuse or a breaker. Individual circuits are connected to the service panel by way of a cable, or separate conductors protected by conduit. Current flows to the device through the "hot" or black wires. Then it returns to the source via the "neutral" or white wires. Control devices, like switches, are always installed in the "hot" leg of the circuit.

Boxes and wiring. Electrical boxes contain and protect devices such as receptacles, switches, and fixtures. The National Electrical Code also requires that all splices be made in, and contained within, an approved metal or plastic box. Boxes may be inset into walls or flush-mounted to a framing member as shown here. Sheathed cables (such as non-metallic cable) can run directly into a box as long as the cable is clamped securely; cable or individual wires may be protected with metal or plastic conduit.

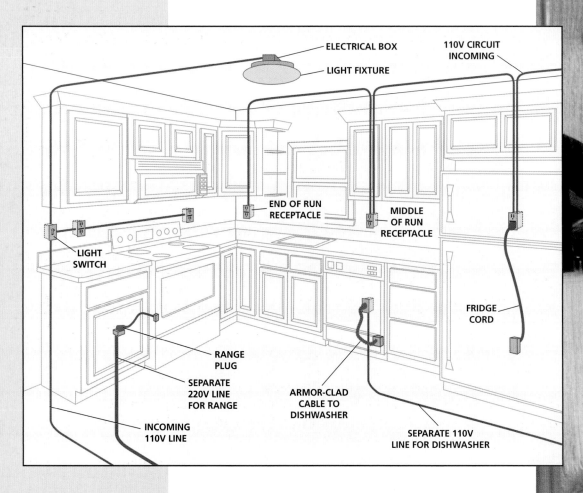

ELECTRICAL BOX

LIGHT FIXTURE

110V CIRCUIT INCOMING

END OF RUN RECEPTACLE

MIDDLE OF RUN RECEPTACLE

LIGHT SWITCH

FRIDGE CORD

RANGE PLUG

SEPARATE 220V LINE FOR RANGE

ARMOR-CLAD CABLE TO DISHWASHER

INCOMING 110V LINE

SEPARATE 110V LINE FOR DISHWASHER

Lighting. Most light fixtures attach directly to electrical boxes—the fixture wires are joined to the circuit and stored within the box. Other fixtures, such as recessed lights, don't require an electrical box for mounting, but they do need one nearby to encase the connections to the electrical circuit. Common light fixtures include incandescent, fluorescent, and halogen—virtually all are controlled by wall-mounted switches.

Switches and receptacles. Switches control the "hot" leg of the circuit. A single-pole switch controls a light fixture from a single location; three-way switches control a light fixture from two locations. Receptacles, or outlets, allow quick and safe access to the power system via any plug-in device. Special GFCI receptacles are now required by code to be installed in all kitchens (see the sidebar below).

Appliances. Electric ranges, cooktops, and ovens require 110- and/or 220-volt receptacles. Some units use 220 for the burners or bake units and 110 for timer, clock, buzzer, and light. The 220 line for these is typically rated 40 to 60 amps. Dishwashers require a dedicated 110-volt, 20-amp line; garbage disposals usually don't require their own line.

GROUND-FAULT CIRCUIT INTERRUPTERS

■ GFCI (ground-fault circuit interrupter) receptacles are safety devices designed to turn off power when a ground fault occurs. During normal operation the current flowing into a circuit or device should be the same as that flowing out of the device or circuit. If they're not the same, some of the current is flowing where it shouldn't, such as when an appliance is faulty, or an accident happens (like dropping a plugged-in mixer in a sink full of water). If the receptacle is GFCI-protected, it will shut off power almost instantaneously. That's why code now requires GFCI-protected receptacles in the kitchen. You don't necessarily have to install GFCI receptacles; you can protect standard receptacles by having a GFCI breaker installed in the service panel (this should be done by a licensed electrician).

VENTILATION SYSTEM

■ The purpose of a mechanical ventilation system in a kitchen is to remove odors, smoke, excess heat, and moisture. It can do this only if the system is designed to match the appliances and is used religiously. Most folks wouldn't consider using a fireplace without opening a damper, but will use a range or cooktop without turning on the vent. There are three basic types of venting commonly found in kitchens: ceiling exhaust, range ventilation, and recirculating systems (see the illustration on the opposite page).

Ceiling exhaust. Ceiling exhaust systems are common in older homes. With these systems, the polluted air is allowed to mix with the house air and is then drawn up into the ceiling exhaust, pushed through a filter, and then quite often vented into the attic space. This is harmful to your attic space, as the grease and contaminants will collect on your framing members and insulation, creating a nasty fire hazard. And, any moisture vented in the attic will eventually cause metal fasteners to rust.

Photo courtesy of Faber

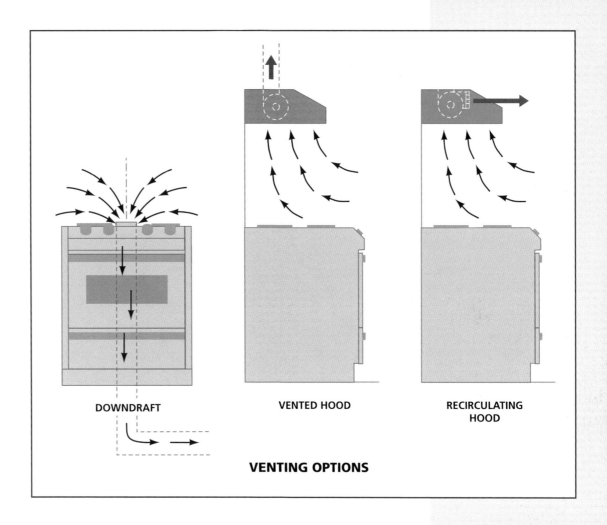

DOWNDRAFT

VENTED HOOD

RECIRCULATING
HOOD

VENTING OPTIONS

Range ventilation. Range ventilation is by far the most common and most successful way to remove pollutants from the kitchen. With this type of system, grease, moisture, and odors are captured at the source, filtered, and then vented outdoors. Range ventilation can be accomplished with overhead hoods or downdraft units. Overhead hoods may be wall-mounted or ceiling-mounted, or may attach to the underside of an overhanging cabinet. Downdraft units are usually an integral part of the range or cooktop and may have a center vent, a side vent, or a pop-up rear vent.

Recirculating systems. Although they're commonly referred to as venting systems, recirculating systems do not vent air. All they do is pull in contaminated air, push it through a filter, and then send it back out into the room. These systems do little if anything to reduce moisture, and their effectiveness is based on how well the filters are maintained. Some include charcoal filters to help remove odors; these filters work only for a short time. If at all possible, a properly ducted range vent should be installed.

Airflow. The size of the vent unit must match the type of range or cooktop. Professional-duty ranges generate high heat and therefore require larger exhaust systems capable of moving a lot of air. Exhaust systems are rated by the volume of air they can move in a minute, in cubic feet per minute (cfm). See the chart below for cfm ratings for typical exhaust systems. Your range or cooktop distributor will be able to tell you what cfm rating the unit will require.

CFM RATING REQUIREMENTS	
Type of unit	**cfm rating**
Downdraft unit	300 to 500
Island hood	400 to 600
Microwave hood	200 to 400
Range hood	150 to 600

VENTILATION SYSTEM, *continued*

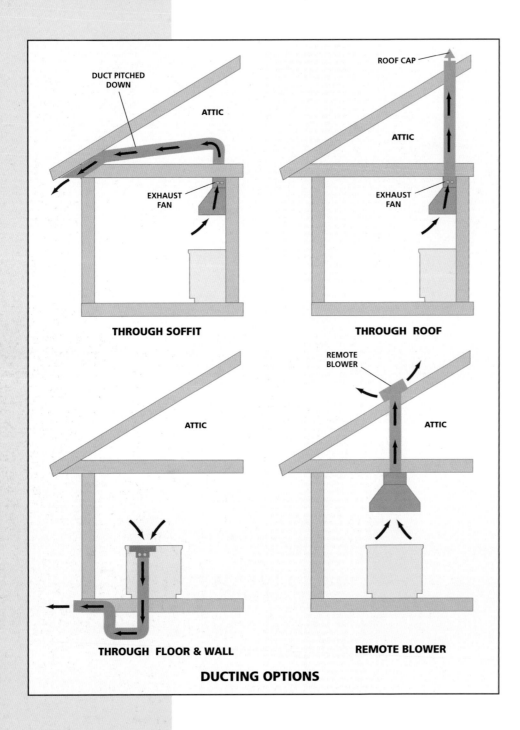

THROUGH SOFFIT

DUCT PITCHED DOWN

ATTIC

EXHAUST FAN

THROUGH ROOF

ROOF CAP

ATTIC

EXHAUST FAN

THROUGH FLOOR & WALL

ATTIC

REMOTE BLOWER

REMOTE BLOWER

ATTIC

DUCTING OPTIONS

Ducting. Matching the exhaust system to the cooktop or range is only half of an effective system. The ducting must be selected and installed properly to vent the polluted air out of the kitchen. In most cases, the ducting will be either 6" round duct or 3" × 10" rectangular duct (both have an internal surface area of 30"). To prevent problems with moisture, this ducting should be aluminum or galvanized and should always be installed so it pitches down toward an external vent—this allows condensation to drain out harmlessly.

The drawing at left illustrates four common ways to route ducting from the hood or downdraft unit to the exterior of the home: over and down through the soffit, up and out the roof, down through the floor and out the wall, and up through the roof using a remote blower.

For maximum efficiency, ducting should be as short as possible and make minimum bends or turns. Do not use flexible plastic ducting (commonly used on clothes dryers), since the hot air will melt the plastic and possibly cause a fire. If you're planning on installing the ducting yourself, avoid venting through the roof—this can cause you headaches as leaks eventually form.

Real Makeover Examples

ORIGINAL KITCHEN

ECONOMY MAKEOVER

MID-RANGE MAKEOVER

HIGH-END MAKEOVER

Since there is no one-size-fits-all solution to a kitchen makeover, this section features different levels of upgrades. So you can see what you get for your dollar, we've made over the same kitchen three times: an economy, a mid-range, and a high-end version. Each "look" was created by Connie Edwards, CKD, CBD, Director of Design for Timberlake Cabinet Company. Our "base point" is the original kitchen, in all its 1970s frumpiness.

Each of the three makeovers includes a photo of the redone kitchen, a top view floor plan, and a photo of the color board we used to define the look (see page 21 for more on color boards).

We offer these makeovers as samples only of what you *might* do, with room for your own tastes and preferences. We'll show you what projects cost and the results you can achieve. Then you can pick and choose the projects for your makeover. Of course, material selection, color, and patterns will vary according to your plans. When you've decided what you want to pursue, advance to Part 3: Creating Your New Look.

THE ORIGINAL KITCHEN

The kitchen we chose as our "lab" for this makeover book was an untouched 1970s original. Everything from the green tortoise-shell laminated countertops to the pale orange flocked wallpaper was the real thing. The new owner had replaced the avocado appliances with white ones, with the exception of the range hood (which we replaced).

The site-built cabinets were still in pretty good shape, but the countertop was near to falling off. A failed seam between the backsplash and the countertop behind the sink had leaked water down the wall and into the floor for years. When it came time for us to lay down new flooring, we ended up ripping out the subfloor down to the joists and installing a new one so we'd have a flat foundation.

Since this wasn't awful enough, the original homeowners had installed a suspended ceiling that was coated with years of grease and grime. We quickly removed this and patched the existing ceiling. This extra space above the cabinets instantly provided a roomier feeling.

As you can see from the floor plan, there was a partial wall that led into the dining room. Unfortunately, this left a space inside the kitchen that was too small for a table and chairs and was mostly wasted.

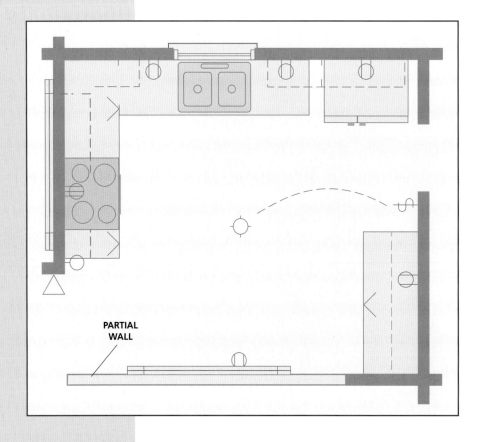

PARTIAL
WALL

AN ECONOMY MAKEOVER

■ For our economy makeover we wanted to update the kitchen to a more contemporary look as inexpensively as possible. To achieve this, we went with cool colors, a moderately bright countertop, and stainless-steel hardware.

We started by stripping the wallpaper and painting the walls. Then we removed the old countertop, painted the cabinets, and added the new hardware. Next we installed a new plastic laminate countertop and added a new stainless-steel sink with a matching faucet.

Finally we applied individual floor tiles and added a snack bar on top of the partial wall to create a cozy eating space. Including the range hood we installed previously, the total cost of the makeover was around $800 (which was for materials only, since we did all the work on this project). Quite an amazing difference for so little money.

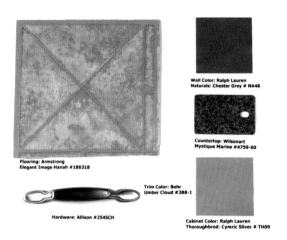

Flooring: Armstrong
Elegant Image Hanah #186318

Hardware: Allison #254SCH

Wall Color: Ralph Lauren
Naturals: Chester Grey # NA48

Countertop: Wilsonart
Mystique Marine #4759-60

Trim Color: Behr
Umber Cloud #388-1

Cabinet Color: Ralph Lauren
Thoroughbred: Cymric Sliver # TH09

Economy color board: Floor tiles in shades of gray and blue veining help blend together the blue-speckled laminate countertop and the light gray cabinets and darker gray walls. Silvery hardware adds to the cool, contemporary look.

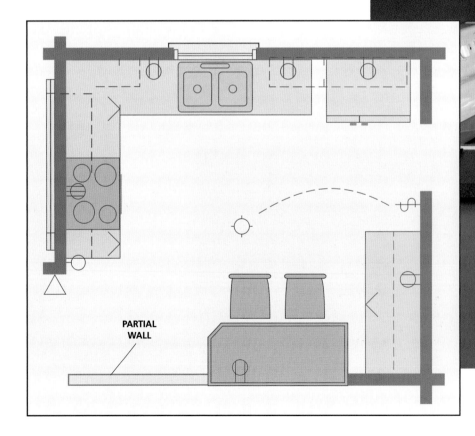

PARTIAL
WALL

WHAT WE DID

Stripped wallpaper ($25)

Painted walls ($50)

Painted kitchen cabinets ($25)

New cabinet hardware ($50)

Installed a post-formed laminate countertop ($100)

New stainless steel sink ($100)

Installed a new faucet: Danze dual-handle faucet ($150)

Individual vinyl floor tiles ($125)

Added a laminate countertop snack bar ($75)

Installed new range hood ($100)

Total cost: $700–$900, depending on materials selected

A Mid-Range Makeover

■ We were after a country look in our mid-range makeover—a very popular theme. The floral wallpaper has a comforting effect and blends well with the other materials. We refaced the existing cabinets with oak, added crown molding, and installed ceramic hardware. The Corian countertop and sink we had professionally installed, but we added the matching faucet and painted the window trim.

To provide a nice accent, we installed a decorative single-tile backsplash and added some under-cabinet lighting. For added storage we installed tilt-out sink trays and installed an under-cabinet wine rack. Since we wanted even more storage, additional counter space, and seating, we removed the partial wall and installed an island and tiled the top. Finally, we installed a laminate floor that offered the look of ceramic tiles but without the mess. Our total cost was $6,290 (not including $450 for the professional installations), but this could vary anywhere from $5,000 to $7,000, depending on materials choices.

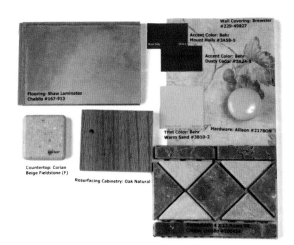

Mid-range color board: Cabinets refaced with red oak and adorned with ivory ceramic knobs set the tone for this country kitchen. Grape-themed wallpaper, a tile backsplash, and the flooring add a dash of color to the otherwise neutral colors.

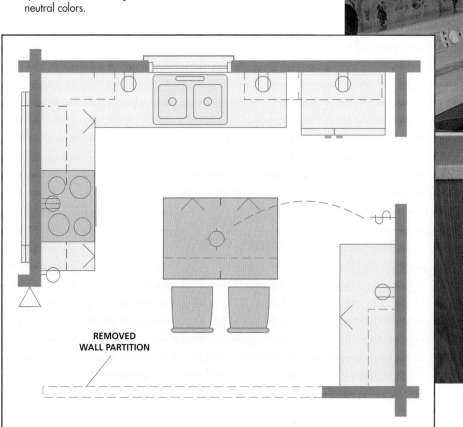

REMOVED WALL PARTITION

WHAT WE DID

Removed wall partition ($0)

Wallpapered walls ($100)

Refaced kitchen cabinets ($2,000)

New cabinet hardware ($100)

Added crown molding ($200)

Painted trim ($15)

Under-cabinet lighting ($35)

Wine storage ($15)

Sink trays ($25)

Corian countertop ($2,100)

Corian sink ($700)

Installed a pullout sprayer unit ($150)

Single-tile backsplash ($100)

Kitchen island ($200)

Laminate flooring ($500)

Installed a ceramic tile countertop ($50)

Total cost: $5,000–$7,000, depending on materials selected

A HIGH-END MAKEOVER

■ We pulled out all the stops—including the old cabinets—in this deluxe makeover. This kitchen is an organic cross between country and contemporary. It features light, warm cabinets, floor, and ceiling, a mid-tone wall, and rich, earthy countertops.

After removing the old cabinets, we added a wall partition (behind the refrigerator) to maximize the space we had to work with (see page 58 for illustrations of this high-end kitchen). The cabinets were professionally installed, and then we added new window trim, pullout bins, and an appliance garage.

The countertop—in this case, top-of-the-line Zodiaq quartz—along with a stainless-steel undermount sink, was also installed professionally, but we installed the wall oven and cooktop ourselves. For lighting we installed recessed cans for general and task lighting, added pendant lights over the peninsula, and added halogen lights under the wall cabinets.

Finally, we installed a garbage disposal and the dishwasher and completed the project by laying a ceramic tile floor. Although the total bill was $26,960 (not including $2,700 for the professional installation of the cabinets, countertop, and sink), you can do it for a lot less by splurging on only one thing, such as cabinets, the countertop, or the appliances. Keep in mind that the Zodiaq countertop alone was $6,000, and the high-end Gaggenau and Bosch appliances we used totaled over $8,000. By using less-expensive versions, you can easily trim $10,000 off the project cost.

High-end color board:
Dramatic brick red walls and a deep brown quartz countertop offset the neutral light maple cabinets and sandy brown tile floor. Dark brown hardware sets off doors and drawers, and stainless steel appliances complete the look.

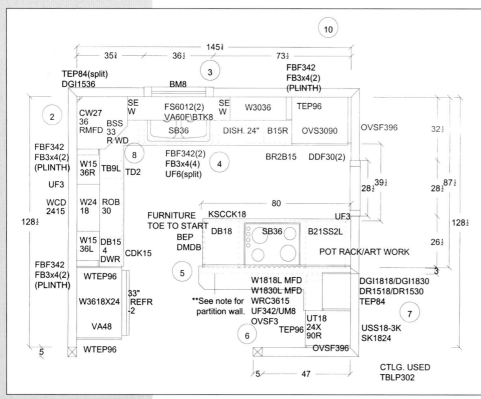

These are some of the drawings provided by the design crew of Timberlake Cabinet Company. At top left is a 3-D view looking into the far left corner of the kitchen. Top right is a 3-D view looking back toward the peninsula, which combines a cooktop with a seating area. The bottom view at left provides an overall view of the new kitchen. If you compare it to the top views of the first two makeovers, you'll see where we removed the partial wall that ran parallel to the window and added a small wall behind where the new refrigerator is installed.

Creating Your New Look

Now that we've looked at planning your improvements, and shown the wide range of prices and possibilities at your disposal, it's time for the fun stuff: making over *your* kitchen.

In part 3, we've organized the makeover projects into six major categories: flooring, cabinets, countertops, walls, plumbing, and electrical. This is a cafeteria-style menu: Pick the project you want to do, and jump right in. To help you visualize the results, each project begins with a photo of the completed work.

As a guide, each makeover project also lists the tools that you'll need and offers detailed, step-by-step instructions, with photography.

KITCHEN FLOORING

Whether it's a big room or a small space, with fancy tile or sheet vinyl, your kitchen floor has two big "musts": durability, since it's the highest-traffic floor in the house, and good looks. And unlike floors in other rooms, the kitchen floor also has to withstand a daily assault of spills from food and water.

With few exceptions, you can install most flooring types yourself by following the guidelines here. We'll cover the most popular—and readily available—types of flooring: sheet vinyl, individual vinyl tiles, ceramic tile, and laminate flooring. Looking for hardwood flooring or carpeting? You won't find them here, because they don't belong in kitchens: Carpeting stains and is tough to clean, and solid hardwood floors warp and twist when exposed to liquids.

Regardless of the floor size or complexity, it's important to draw a rough plan of the room so that a flooring supplier can help you order the correct amount of flooring. You don't need a work of art, just a sketch with accurate dimensions and door openings.

4

Foundations

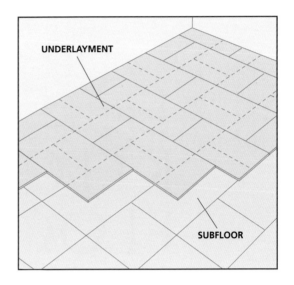

Regardless of the material chosen as the top layer, the underlying structure of floors is similar. The most common type in residential construction is the framed floor (bottom drawing). On a ground-level framed floor, the flooring rests on joists that sit on sills along the foundation; it's often supported at a midpoint by a girder. An elevated framed floor like the one shown is supported by beams that run perpendicular to the joists, where the floor's weight is borne by support columns. In most cases, the joists are tied together with bridging for extra stability and to prevent them from moving sideways.

The joists are covered with some form of sub-flooring, typically tongue-and-groove plywood, particleboard, or OSB (oriented-strand board). Depending on the type of flooring used, the subfloor may be covered with an additional layer of underlayment, such as $1/4$" plywood (typically Lauan) or cement board. The actual flooring is then installed on top of the underlayment or subfloor and may or may not rest on a cushioning layer, such as roofing felt.

A very common question about flooring is whether you'll have to remove the old before installing the new. The answer depends on the type and condition of your existing floor. If the subfloor is sturdy and level, you can usually install a new layer over the existing layer—this is particularly true with vinyl flooring. If the subfloor is sturdy but not level, adding a new layer of underlayment is a great way to create a flat reference surface. Note: To prevent cracks in the new flooring, it's important that seams of the underlayment don't match up with seams in the subfloor. Cut the underlayment as necessary to prevent this from happening (top drawing).

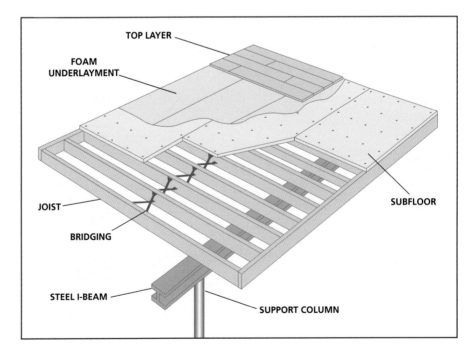

Sheet Vinyl Flooring

Sheet vinyl flooring is one of the best all-around flooring choices for a kitchen. It's inexpensive, durable, and easy to install, and it comes in many patterns and colors. And, most quality vinyl flooring comes with a built-in cushion to make it easy on your feet. The problem is that when many people think of sheet vinyl, an image of '50s linoleum pops into their heads. Although often hideous, that old linoleum was virtually impervious to wear. Today's sheet vinyl flooring is just as tough, and what makes it even better is that its no-wax finish is incredibly easy to clean and maintain.

Full-adhesive. There are two common ways to install sheet vinyl: full-adhesive and perimeter install. Sheet vinyl flooring that's attached to the entire subfloor with adhesive is referred to as a full-adhesive installation. Since the flooring is firmly glued to the subfloor, it's very durable. This is espe-cially true if it's a single piece; without seams, it's impossible for water, dirt, and dust to sneak under it to weaken the glue bond.

Perimeter install. On a perimeter install, the flooring is attached only around the perimeter with staples. The rest of the flooring "floats" on the sub-floor. The advantage to this is that it's not as messy as a full-adhesive installation. The disadvantage? Since most of the flooring isn't attached, it can tear or rip easily—even high-heeled shoes can damage it. Also, since most perimeter-installed sheet vinyl is stretched slightly as it's attached, a knife dropped in the kitchen can puncture the flooring, often creat-ing a large rip.

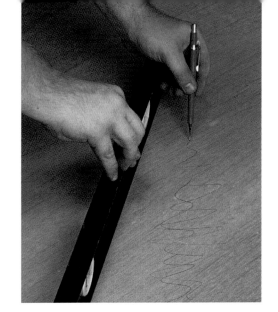

Install new underlayment. If your existing floor isn't level or is damaged, it's best to add new underlayment to provide a flat gluing surface. To do this, begin by fastening sheets in one corner, and work your way across the room. Cut sheets as necessary to prevent overlapping the seams in the subfloor (see page 62). Fasten the underlayment to the subfloor every 6" along the edges and at 8" to 12" intervals throughout the sheet. Use screws, staples, or ring-shank nails.

Check for level. To check your subfloor, slide a 4-foot level along the surface. A low-angle light (such as a trouble light) placed on the opposite side will help you clearly see highs and lows. When you detect a problem area, mark a rough outline on the floor to indicate its general shape. High spots are taken care of by refastening the subfloor to the joists or by sanding off the peaks with a belt sander fitted with a coarse-grit belt.

Apply leveling compound. Floor levelers are mortar-like cement-based coatings that go down smoothly and set up quickly. Mix according to the manufacturer's directions, and apply it to the floor with a flat-edged trowel (right). Instead of one thick coat, trowel on multiple thin coats, carefully feathering the edges. When the leveler is dry, scrape off any

ridges or high spots with a sharp putty knife and then recheck with the 4-foot level. Repeat as necessary to fill in all depressions.

In addition to leveling out low spots in a subfloor, levelers are a great way to prevent old embossed flooring from imprinting its pattern over time onto a new flooring, such as resilient sheet vinyl. A thin coat of leveler will fill in all the indentations in the old tile to prevent this (inset below).

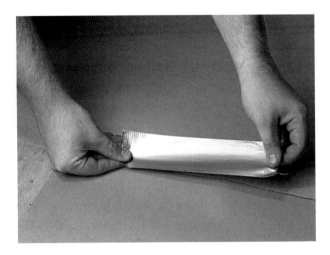

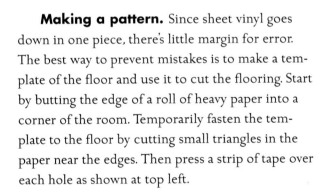

Making a pattern. Since sheet vinyl goes down in one piece, there's little margin for error. The best way to prevent mistakes is to make a template of the floor and use it to cut the flooring. Start by butting the edge of a roll of heavy paper into a corner of the room. Temporarily fasten the template to the floor by cutting small triangles in the paper near the edges. Then press a strip of tape over each hole as shown at top left.

Work around the perimeter. Continue rolling paper along the perimeter of the room. Overlap the pieces 2", and fasten them at the seams (above). Cut triangular holes in the paper as you did for the first strip, and fasten each to the floor as you

work. Butt the edges of the paper as close as possible to the wall. If there's more than a $1/4$" gap between the paper and the wall, trim the paper so it fits snugly.

Mark around obstacles. When you come to an obstacle (such as a pipe), you'll need to fit the template around it. One way to do this is to "scribe" around the obstacle with a compass. Place the paper as close as possible to the wall, then open a compass so it spans the largest gap between the paper and wall. Place the pencil on the paper and press the point of the compass against the wall. As you guide the compass along the wall, the pencil will copy the irregularities directly onto the paper (top right).

Transfer the template to the flooring.
Next, unroll the template onto the flooring and temporarily fasten it in place. For floors that require pieces to be joined, overlap the pieces and tape them together. Position the pieces so that the pattern flows perfectly from one piece to the other. As you position the template, take care to adjust its position so it's centered on the pattern and the pattern is as equal as possible on all sides.

Cut the flooring to size. Once the template is fastened to the flooring correctly, you can cut it to match the template. Start by making the straight perimeter cuts with a utility knife, using a metal straightedge as a guide (top right). Slide a scrap of plywood underneath to protect the existing floor. Then make your obstacle cuts. For intricate curves, make a series of light cuts instead of one heavy one.

Trowel on the adhesive. If you're working with one piece, pull one side back toward the cen-

ter and apply flooring adhesive with the recommended notched trowel. Then unfold it back into position. Repeat this process for the other half. If you're working with multiple pieces, use this same process, except do this for each piece. It's best to roll and press one piece in place at a time. This gives the other piece a solid edge to butt up against—there's just a lot less slipping and sliding this way.

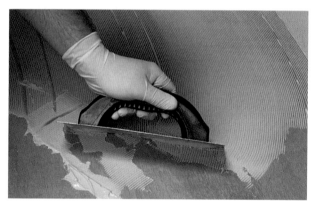

PERIMETER INSTALLATIONS

■ On perimeter installs, pull the flooring tight against the wall and staple it to the subfloor about every 2". Work around the room, pulling and stapling. Keep the staples as near to the wall as possible. They'll be covered later when you install cove base molding or other trim. You should also apply adhesive under the flooring near an obstacle to help keep it flat, and under the first 6" to 8" around a door threshold. Although this area is stapled as well, the adhesive helps prevent the flooring from stretching too much under the constant barrage of foot traffic.

Press flooring in place. The next very important step is to firmly press the flooring in place to get a good glue bond. A rental tool called a flooring roller is used for this—if you skip this, you'll likely be plagued with air bubbles and loose sections. A 75- or 100-pound roller rents for less than $20 a day in most areas. Begin rolling in the center of the room, working your way toward the wall. This pushes out air bubbles so they can escape and moves any excess adhesive to the edges, where it can be removed.

WORKING WITH SEAMS

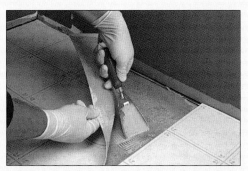

Apply adhesive. In large kitchens, you may need to seam together sheets of vinyl flooring. Regardless of whether it's a full-adhesive or perimeter installation, you must apply adhesive under both sides of the seam. This is a given with full-adhesive installations, but with perimeter installs, you'll need to apply a strip of adhesive about 6" to 8" on both sides of the seam. That's because you can't use staples here—they'd be visible. Instead, you have to rely on the adhesive.

Roll the seam. After the adhesive is applied, fold back each section of flooring and press the edges together to form a tight seam. Use a small hand roller, rolling pin, or laminate roller to press the flooring firmly into the adhesive. Wipe up any squeeze-out with a soft cloth dampened in solvent. Strips of duct tape applied across the seam every 4" to 6" will help hold it together until it has set up.

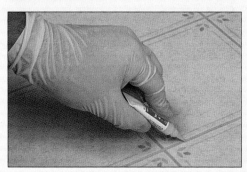

Seal the seam. After the adhesive has set, seal the seam using the sealer recommended by the manufacturer of the sheet vinyl. Most of these fuse the edges of the sheet vinyl together to create a leak-proof seal. Make sure to follow the manufacturer's instructions to the letter. If you don't, you may void the warranty.

Individual Tiles

Ease of installation is the beauty of vinyl tiles. Unlike installing sheet vinyl flooring, where you often have to struggle with large, heavy, and awkward sheets, 12" squares seem blissfully workable. Small square tiles are a lot easier to maneuver—especially when you're working around an obstacle like a set of pipes or a piece of conduit.

Unfortunately, individual vinyl tiles have suffered from a poor reputation for the last decade or so. The main culprit? Self-adhesive tile. It seemed like such a good idea—just peel off the backing and press the tile in place for a new floor—that lots of homeowners gave it try. Many were severely disappointed, for several reasons. To allow the tiles to conform to uneven floors, manufacturers made the tiles thin. This made them prone to cracking, chipping, and dents. Also, adhesives at the time weren't as strong as today's glues, and the bond between floor and tile often failed. Fortunately, with advances in both plastics and adhesives, modern vinyl tiles are both flexible and durable.

The secret to successfully installing vinyl tiles is the subfloor. Since there are so many seams with vinyl tiles, the subfloor needs to be really flat and free of debris. Even a small piece of sawdust trapped under a vinyl tile can cause the tile to crack over time or can weaken the adhesive bond. Take care to scrape the subfloor to remove any old residue and carefully vacuum the floor before applying adhesive.

Test tile placement. To keep from having narrow tiles at the perimeter of the room, temporarily set out a row of tiles, starting at the centerpoint and working toward the walls. If you find a narrow gap between the last full tile and the wall on either end,

shift the appropriate centerline to eliminate it. Repeat this process for the opposite direction to make sure you don't have any narrow tiles on the remaining walls.

Snap reference lines. Once you've located your starting points, use a chalk line to snap a reference line, making sure it's parallel to the wall. Then locate the center of the line you just snapped (or the offset mark if you adjusted the location to compensate for narrow end tiles), and use a framing square to lay out a line perpendicular to this.

Adhesive choices. To install a self-adhesive tile, start by peeling off the protective paper backing. Since you'll be accumulating a lot of waste with the backing, it's a good idea to have a helper handy to collect and dispose of it. If you're using flooring adhesive to affix the tiles, start at the intersection of the reference lines and apply adhesive with a notched trowel to one quadrant (inset below). Hold the trowel at approximately a 45-degree angle as you spread the adhesive, and apply it until you reach one wall.

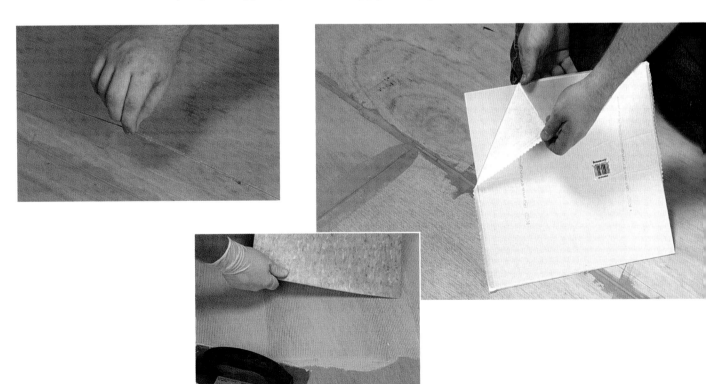

Apply the tiles. Carefully set a row of tiles along one of the reference lines. Don't slide the tiles into place; instead, drop them into position. Then set a row of tiles perpendicular to the first row you laid down. Next, fill in the quadrant between the two outer rows. Note: Most tiles have an arrow printed on the back to indicate which direction they should be laid. Make sure that all the arrows are facing the same direction as you install the tiles.

Mark and cut partial tiles. After you've installed all the full tiles, you can add the border tiles. To mark a tile for cutting, place a tile on the nearest full tile to the wall. Then set a $1/8"$ spacer against the wall and place a "marker" tile on top of the tile to be cut, and slide the marker tile until it butts against the spacer. Next, using the edge of the marker tile as a guide, draw a line on the tile (see page 74). Now you can cut the bottom tile to fit.

Press tiles in place. To create the best bond between the subfloor and the tile, the tiles need to be firmly and evenly pressed into the flooring adhesive. Here again, the best tool for this job is a flooring roller, available at most rental centers. Thin tile can be pressed with a 70-pound roller; thicker tiles (such as rubber tiles) are best pressed in place with a 100-pound roller.

Once you've got one quadrant laid down and pressed, repeat for the three remaining quadrants.

INSTALLING A METAL THRESHOLD

■ To protect the edges of the sheet flooring at the door thresholds, install metal transition strips. To do this, measure the door opening and cut the transition strip to length with metal snips or a hacksaw. Then attach the strip to the subfloor with the nails provided. Home centers carry transition strips in standard door widths in a variety of colors. These strips let you handle the transition from just about any type of flooring to another.

Installing Cove Base

TOOLS
- Utility knife or shears
- Straightedge
- Notched knife or trowel

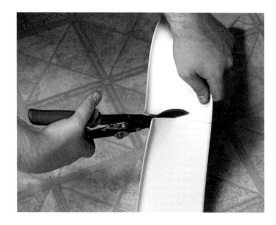

Vinyl cove base is the perfect trim for many floors— it goes particularly well with vinyl. It's easy to work with, goes on fast, and comes in many colors. Cove base is available in rolls and strips. Roll molding can save you a lot of time making seams; it's the best choice for large rooms. Although strip molding requires seams, its short lengths make it easier to work with.

adhesive to the back of the cove base instead of onto the wall. Spread adhesive onto the back of the molding with a notched knife or trowel. To avoid squeeze-out, keep the adhesive about $1/2$" from the top edge.

Positioning cove base. Read and follow the manufacturer's instructions on how much time (if any) you should allow for the adhesive to set up (or get tacky) before installing the cove base. When it's ready, position it near the wall with the curved lip at the bottom, resting on the floor. Then tilt the molding up until it rests against the wall. Press it firmly in place with your hand, working from one edge of the strip to the opposite edge.

Cutting cove base. All it takes to work with cove base molding is a sharp utility knife, a notched trowel, and some cove base adhesive. Whenever possible, use water-based adhesive: It's much easier to clean up than the solvent-based varieties. To cut cove base, use a sharp utility knife and a straightedge. Alternatively, a pair of heavy-duty shears will do the job.

Back-buttering. The tidiest way to apply adhesive to cove base is to use a technique called "back-buttering." With this method you apply the

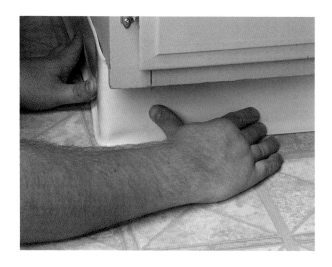

Ceramic Tile Flooring

Ceramic floor tile doesn't deserve its bad reputation for being difficult to install. Sure, it's a bit more complicated than other flooring materials, and it certainly takes longer (mainly because you have to wait for materials to set up, like the mortar that holds the tile to the floor and the grout that fills the spaces between the tiles). But if you break each of the tasks down into simple steps, it's really pretty easy.

After you've chosen the tile for your floor, the next step is to establish what type of pattern you want. The best way to visualize what will look best is to lay a row or two of tiles on the floor. Try a square pattern, or possibly one where the tiles are oriented diagonally to the corners of the room. Remember to leave a space between the tiles roughly equivalent to the size of the grout joint you've chosen. Better yet, insert the actual spacers between the tiles as you lay them down.

Here's how to avoid making a common costly mistake (it's a pro tip from flooring contractors): Once your reference lines are snapped, take the time to make a final dry test of the entire pattern to make sure the tiles fit as planned.

When you've decided on a pattern, check to make sure that your floor is level. Set a 3- or 4-foot-long level on the tiles or subfloor and check it for level at several places around the room.

A common floor tiling mistake is to ignore the border tiles that are cut to fit around the perimeter of the room. To prevent narrow tiles, draw your tile pattern on a piece of graph paper to scale. Then on tracing paper, draw the outline of the room to scale. Now place the tracing paper over the tile pattern and move it around to produce the fewest narrow tiles. Then note how much you'll need to offset the reference lines that you'll use to install the tiles from true center.

Install cement board. Because they're brittle, ceramic tiles need an underlayment that won't flex. The underlayment also must be impervious to moisture. The solution is cement board. It comes in 32" × 60" sheets and is $1/2$" thick. Attach cement board to the existing subfloor with thin-set mortar and screws. Secure it every 6" along the edges and every 8" throughout the interior. Then apply mesh tape over the seams and spread a layer of mortar over the tape with a putty knife (inset).

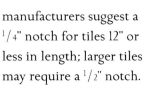

Add battens. Although not absolutely necessary, it's a good idea to install battens (1×2s) as a solid starting point for each quadrant—they're especially useful if this is your first time laying tile. Battens not only help ensure alignment, but they also help prevent the tiles from sliding around in thin-set mortar. The battens are just straight 1×2s that you align with the reference marks you made earlier, then fasten to the subfloor—one per side (below).

Apply mortar. Mix up enough thin-set mortar to cover one of the quadrants. Then use a square-notched trowel to spread the mortar all the way up to the battens or reference lines (bottom right). Most thin-set mortar manufacturers suggest a $1/4$" notch for tiles 12" or less in length; larger tiles may require a $1/2$" notch. Avoid working the mortar excessively on the subfloor. What you're looking for here is a consistent layer of mortar with no bare spots.

Apply grout. Before you apply grout, remove any plastic spacers. Mix up only enough grout to work a small section of tile at a time. This not only allows you to take your time to do the job right, but also makes mixing easier, since you're working with smaller batches. Start in a corner and pour some grout on the tile. Use a grout float to force the grout into the joints. Then hold the float diagonally and at an angle to skim off the excess, as shown below.

Position tiles. Start by setting a tile in the corner where the battens meet. Press down as you lay the tile to force it into the mortar. As soon as the tile is down, "set" it in the mortar by tapping it with a soft rubber-faced mallet; this makes the mortar spread evenly to give the best grip possible. Continue laying tiles along both reference lines, then fill in the quadrant and remove the battens. To ensure consistent spacing, insert cross-shaped plastic tile spacers between each tile as shown above.

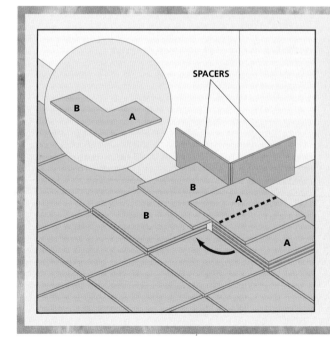

SPACERS

WORKING AROUND CORNERS

■ Partial tiles, where you need to cut a notch to fit around an outside corner or other obstacle, are a bit tricky. You can use the same procedure to mark the tile as discussed for vinyl tiles on page 70. The only difference is you have to set up and mark the tile on both sides of the corner. Remember to insert a spacer between the wall and the tile equal to the thickness of one grout line.

Clean the tile. Although removing the remaining grout from the tiles with a sponge is easy work, it takes time. Have a large bucket of water on hand, and refill it with clean water often. Just as you did with the float, wipe the sponge diagonally over the tiles (below). Wipe over each grout joint only once; repeated wiping can pull the grout out of the joint. After the grout has dried for about 4 to 6 hours, use a soft cloth to wipe away any haze (inset).

Tooling grout. Some tile manufacturers suggest that you "tool" the grout joints for uniform appearance. Although you can purchase a special tool for this, a short length of dowel will do. The diameter of the dowel must be large enough to span the joint. The larger its diameter, the smaller the concave depression it'll make in the grout. To use the dowel, position it over a grout joint and draw it along the tile with gentle pressure (bottom left).

Apply sealer. Grout is porous and needs to be sealed to prevent staining and mildew from growing. Following the manufacturer's directions, apply seam sealer to the cured grout. To prevent the sealant from trapping moisture in the grout, most manufacturers suggest waiting 2 to 4 weeks before applying their product. Apply the sealer carefully to the grout joints only with a sponge or sash brush (bottom right). Wipe up any excess sealer immediately with a clean, dry rag.

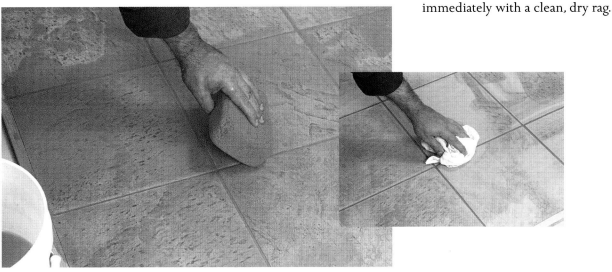

Laminate Flooring

A lot of home-owners were skeptical when they first heard of laminate flooring. The concept of a "floating" floor that doesn't get nailed or fastened to the subfloor made them nervous. What would keep it from buckling or moving around over time? And it's so thin, how could it possibly be durable? But when installed properly, laminate flooring doesn't buckle—it lies perfectly flat. And it's made of materials similar to those used to make the nearly indestructible plastic laminate (like fiberboard, cellulose paper, and hard melamine resins). One of the extra benefits to laminate flooring is it can be laid down over most existing flooring. Not having to first remove the old flooring will save you both time and money. (Note: It shouldn't be laid over carpeting; remove the carpeting first.)

Also, since the planks are glued together, you effectively create one large panel that can swell or shrink as a single unit when humidity changes.

Here's where not attaching it to the subfloor is a benefit: The flooring can expand or contract without buckling, unlike hardwood flooring.

Important: The first three rows, or "starter course," of laminate flooring is critical to the overall success of the installation. These planks must go down flat and straight so that the rest of the planks will be easy to install. To make sure everything fits well, it's best to "dry-fit" the planks together before applying glue.

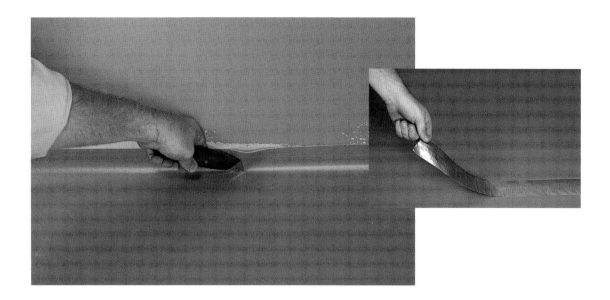

Install an underlayment. All laminate flooring needs underlayment to deaden sound, prevent glue from adhering the planks to the subfloor, and cushion your step; the most common of these is foam. To install it, place the cut end of the roll against the wall in one corner of the room and unroll it; cut it to length with a sharp utility knife. Butt the edges of the foam together and use duct tape to join the seams.

Create an expansion gap. Starting in one corner, lay down a "plank" with the groove facing the wall. Insert spacers between the plank and the wall to create the appropriate expansion gap; this gap allows the floor to "move" as humidity changes. This gap is typically $1/4$"; you can use scraps of $1/4$"-thick plywood or the plastic spacers that come in most installation kits (as shown here).

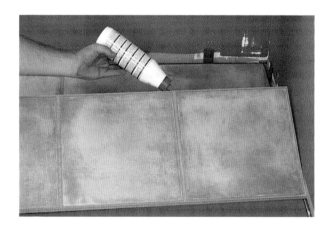

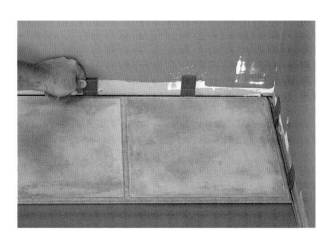

Apply glue to edges and ends. Assemble the first three rows without glue. Follow the instructions on how to stagger the joints. Typically, the first plank in the second row is cut to two-thirds the length of a full plank. The first plank in the third row is one-third of a full plank. When everything fits, slide the planks apart, keeping them in order, and apply glue to one row at a time. Put glue on the side and edge of each plank, unless the edge butts up against a wall.

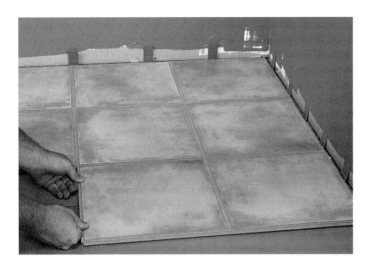

Set the second and third course. As you glue the planks of the first three rows, press the planks together with hand pressure and wipe up any glue squeeze-out with a clean cloth. Don't scrimp on glue here. The last thing you want on a kitchen floor is a seam that isn't watertight. If moisture seeps into the seam, the flooring will swell. That's because the core of laminate flooring is particleboard, which will soak up moisture like a sponge.

Apply clamps to first three rows. As mentioned earlier, the first three courses are the key. Use strap clamps to hold the planks together so the glue can set up (about an hour). You can usually rent an installation kit where you purchased your

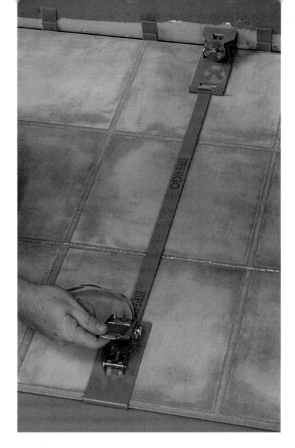

flooring. It'll contain 6 to 10 strap clamps, a tapping block, and spacers. Slip one end of the clamp over the plank near the wall. Fit the end with the ratchet lever over the opposite side. Remove any slack from the strap and ratchet the lever to pull the joints tight.

Wipe away excess glue. As you tighten the clamps, you should experience quite a bit of glue squeeze-out. It's best to remove this immediately with a damp cloth. Have a bucket of clean water handy to periodically rinse out the cloth. After the entire floor is down and you've waited 12 hours for the glue to set up, go over the floor with a damp mop to remove the glue haze.

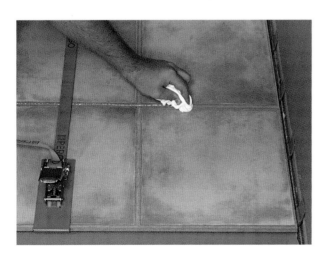

Cutting planks to fit. To cut a plank to fit around an obstacle, clamp the plank face up on a sawhorse or other work surface. You can cut laminate flooring to length with a power miter saw or circular saw. But to cut intricate details, you'll need a saber saw or coping saw. If your saber saw has an orbital action (like the one shown here), turn it off to prevent the aggressive orbital action from tearing the laminate's surface.

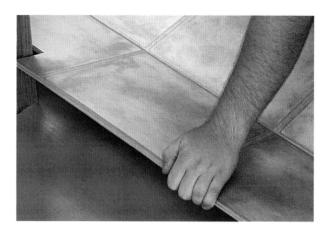

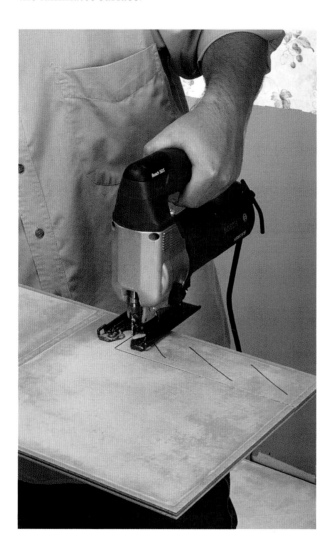

Maintain expansion gap. To allow laminate flooring to wrap around an obstacle (such as a pipe or cabinet), start by cutting a plank to length to fit between the last plank installed and the wall. The important thing here is to remember to subtract $1/4$" for the expansion gap. Then measure and mark the obstacle on the plank.

Cover expansion gap with trim. Most manufacturers of laminate flooring sell base molding that matches their product to cover the expansion gap between the flooring and the wall. Following the manufacturer's instructions, cut the molding to fit and attach as described. Alternatively, you can cover the gap with cove base (as shown here) or any other base molding. (For more on cove base, see page 71.)

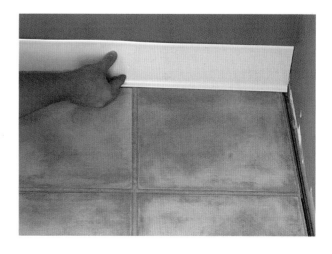

Photo courtesy of American Woodmark

5

KITCHEN CABINETS

Cabinets are the highest-ticket items in your kitchen, but they don't have to be the most expensive part of your makeover. While many people assume they need to completely replace their old cabinets in favor of new units, you can get a totally new look without starting all over. If your existing cabinets are built well and you just want a cosmetic change, you can repaint or reface them. If your heart is set on all-new cabinets, we'll show you how to spend smart there, too.

What do you want your cabinets to do? Basically, to store things and keep them within easy reach. They also need to stand up to daily use: banging, slamming, smeary handprints, food spills, and the like. On top of all that, cabinets are the focal point of the kitchen, and naturally you want them to look good. Here's how to turn your old cabinets into star performers on any budget.

Painting Kitchen Cabinets

The effect of a coat of paint can be astonishing. Just look at the difference between the cabinets in the kitchens shown on pages 50 and 52. Much of the new look came from painting the old, dark cabinets a cooler, more contemporary gray. Whatever color you choose, painting kitchen cabinets is easy and inexpensive and can be accomplished in a weekend.

Before you break out the brushes and rollers, you need to know that only certain kinds of cabinets can be painted. Wood and metal cabinets accept paint well; cabinets where the doors, drawers, and face frames are covered with any kind of plastic laminate (such as melamine) cannot be painted. The same thing that keeps these cabinets from staining also prevents them from accepting paint. If you're not sure, you can check by brushing on a bit of paint in an inconspicuous spot (like the back of a door). When dry, try to scrape off the paint with your fingernail. If the door is covered with plastic laminate, the paint will flake right off.

Remove doors and drawers. The first step in painting cabinets is to remove the doors, drawers, and hardware. Since there will be many parts, label each so you'll know where to re-install. A nifty way to do this on doors is to scratch a reference number under the hinge with a scratch awl. This way you'll be able to read it even after it has been painted—and the hinge will cover the mark when installed. Label drawers by writing numbers on masking tape stuck to the drawer bottoms. Remove the knobs, pulls, hinges, and catches.

Clean and sand. Although you may be anxious to start painting, take the time to prepare the cabinet surfaces so you'll get the best paint bond possible. Start by cleaning the doors, drawer fronts, and face frames with a solution of tri-sodium phosphate (TSP) and water. When dry, sand all surfaces lightly with 150-grit open-coat sandpaper to roughen up the surface enough to give the paint something to "bite" into. Then fill any holes or imperfections with wood filler, let dry, and sand smooth. (Note: If you're reusing hardware, leave the holes for the screws unfilled.)

Paint frames, doors, and drawers. Now you can break out the paint. Begin with a coat of primer on all surfaces. A small foam roller works great for applying primer to the face frames; it works equally well on the drawer fronts and doors. Start with the backs of the doors and, while they're drying, prime the face frames and drawer fronts. When you're done with those, go back and flip the doors over (assuming they're dry) and prime the fronts. Allow the primer to dry overnight and then use the same procedure to paint the face frames, doors, and drawer fronts with the finish coat.

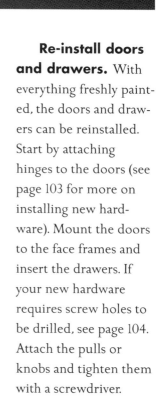

Re-install doors and drawers. With everything freshly painted, the doors and drawers can be reinstalled. Start by attaching hinges to the doors (see page 103 for more on installing new hardware). Mount the doors to the face frames and insert the drawers. If your new hardware requires screw holes to be drilled, see page 104. Attach the pulls or knobs and tighten them with a screwdriver.

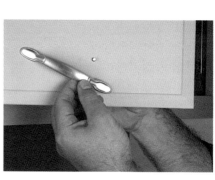

Refacing Kitchen Cabinets

TOOLS

- Tape measure
- Scissors and utility knife
- Screwdriver and hammer
- Try or combination square
- Veneer applicator
- Saber saw
- Sanding block and hand plane
- Putty knife
- Hand saw or laminate trimmer

You've decided it's time for new kitchen cabinets. The big question is, do you want new cabinets, or a new look? If all you're after is a facelift, why not reface your existing cabinets? Refacing is an excellent choice for a number of reasons. It's a whole lot cheaper than replacing—by a factor of 5 or more. And outside of the weekend it takes you to do the actual refacing, it won't disrupt your life the way installing new cabinets does. Add to this the fact that it's easy to do—almost fun—and you'll be looking around at the other cabinets in your home wondering what they'd look like in oak...or maybe maple....

Refacing cabinets consists of replacing the old doors and drawer fronts with new parts and applying wood veneer or plastic laminate over the face frames. The results are amazing—just compare the kitchens on pages 52 and 54. Refacing supplies (doors, drawer fronts, matching end panels, peel-n-stick veneer—even crown molding) can be ordered from most home centers; material choices typically include oak and maple in a variety of finishes, plus white melamine. We used materials supplied by Quality Doors and were impressed with both the product and the ease of installation.

The only requirement for a refacing job is that your old cabinets must be in good structural condition. They can look awful but must be sound: Any surface veneers must be firmly attached, and joints where face frame parts connect together must be flush and secure. That's because any surface imperfections will telegraph through the new veneer.

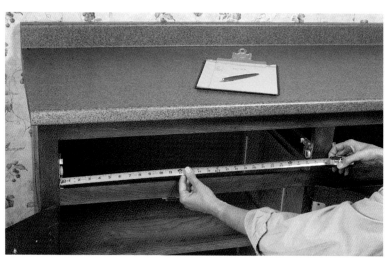

Measure cabinets and order parts.

Before you can begin work on refacing your cabinets, you'll need to measure them so that you can order parts. Follow the manufacturer's instructions; typically this involves measuring the drawer and door openings with a tape measure and making a list. Then you add a set width for overhang. You'll also need to specify how much veneer you'll need and any specialty items such as crown molding and end panels. Double-check each measurement, fill out the form, and place the order.

Remove doors and drawers.

Once the parts have arrived and you're ready to begin work, start by removing the old doors and drawers. Label the drawers so you know where they go back. If the drawers have false fronts (see page 88 for more on this), remove these as well. Loosen and remove all hardware, including pulls, knobs, hinges, and catches. Set aside those you'll reuse.

Prepare face frames.

To ensure that the veneer or laminate bonds securely to the face frames, they need to be free from grease and dirt. Clean the face frames with mild dishwashing detergent and water. Use a damp rag only; do not soak the wood. Rinse with clean water, and when dry, fill any screw holes and imperfections with wood filler or spackling compound. Sand the filler flush when it's totally dry.

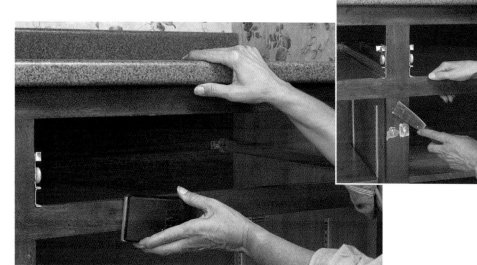

Cut veneer strips to size. It's best to cut veneer strips for one opening at a time. Measure the length and width of one section of the face frame, and cut strips $1/2$" wider and 2" longer. Peel-n-stick veneer is easy to cut with sharp scissors or a utility knife and a straightedge.

END PANELS

■ Before you apply any veneer to the face frames, you'll need to treat the exposed sides of the existing cabinets. These are covered with pieces of $1/4$" matching plywood. If the face frames of your old cabinets are flush with the exposed sides of the cabinets, installation is just a matter of cutting a plywood end panel to match and attaching it with glue and nails. If, however, the face frames extend past the ends (typically $1/4$" or so), you'll need to trim these flush with the ends. This will allow you to attach the plywood end panels flush with the face frame. Then, when the veneer strips are applied to the face frame, these will cover the exposed edge of the plywood.

Trim ends flush. To prepare a cabinet side for a plywood end panel, start by trimming the face frame flush with the cabinet side. A hand plane or a router fitted with a flush-trim bit works well for this.

Cut to fit and attach. Next, cut the plywood end panel to match the side of the cabinet. Attach the plywood panel to the cabinet side with glue and $3/4$"-long brads. A clamp is useful for holding the panel in place while the brads are driven in.

Sand edges flush. Finally, use a sanding block fitted with 120-grit sandpaper to sand the plywood panel flush with the face frame.

CREATING PERFECT SEAMS

■ Here's how to create perfect seams between the rails and the stiles. Start by trimming the excess overlap inside the opening from both stiles and rails. Use the inside of the frame as a guide.

Cut through both layers at once. Position a try square or combination square so the edge is directly over where the rail joins the stile. Now cut through both layers at once with a utility knife.

Remove waste. Then use the tip of the knife to lift up the cut end of the veneer and pry out the waste piece underneath. Press the rail veneer back in place for a perfect seam.

Sand edges flush. Finally, sand the edges of the veneer with a sanding block to make them flush with the inside faces of the cabinet.

Apply veneer to stiles. First, a little lingo: The vertical parts of a cabinet frame are the *stiles;* the horizontal pieces are *rails*. Start by applying veneer to the stiles of the base cabinets. Peel off the backing and carefully position the strip with the top butted up against the countertop. Make sure the veneer extends out equally past each side of the stile. When it's in position, press the veneer firmly into the stile. Most refacing manufacturers sell a special applicator that does a good job of exerting sufficient pressure (photo at right).

Apply veneer to rails. Now you can veneer the rails. Peel off a couple of inches of the backing from a strip and position one end so it overlaps the stile about 1". Align the strip on the face frame so there's an even overlap on the top and bottom of the rail. Then press down and smooth out the strip, working toward the other end, peeling the backing off as you go. Use the applicator to press the veneer firmly in place and then trim any excess off the bottom of the stiles with a utility knife; take several light passes to cut through the veneer (inset).

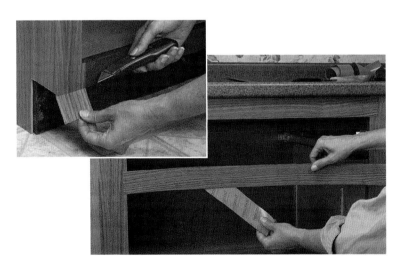

DRAWERS

◼ How easy or difficult it will be to reface your drawers depends on how they're constructed: three-sided or four-sided. If the drawer front makes the forward wall of the drawer, it's three-sided. When the drawer front attaches to a separate piece that makes up the forward wall, the drawer is four-sided.

THREE-SIDED DRAWERS

Since the front of a three-sided drawer is an integral part of the drawer, you can't simply remove it. Instead, you'll need to remove any lips that extend out past the sides so the drawer will fit in the opening, with the front flush with the face frame of the cabinet. This allows you to attach the new front to the drawer—this is often called a false front. Then, depending on the drawer slides, you may be able to swap the drawer's slides between the left and right side and turn the drawer around to hide the cut edges.

Remove drawer lips. To allow the drawer to fit in the opening so it's flush with the face frame, cut the lips off the drawer with a hand saw and smooth the rough edges with a sanding block.

Power trimming. A laminate trimmer fitted with a flush-trim bit will make quick work of removing the drawer lips. It will even cut out notches for drawer glides, as shown here.

FOUR-SIDED DRAWERS

Remove false front. If you're lucky and your cabinet drawers are four-sided, simply remove the screws that hold the front in place. On some drawers, the false front is attached with brads.

Attach new false front. Now you can attach the new front. Take care to center the front from side to side and top to bottom before securing it with screws.

Attach hinges. All that's left is the doors. Unpack the doors and set each in front of the appropriate cabinet opening. Start by attaching the hinges. A slick way to do this is with a combination square. Set the blade of the square so it extends out the distance you want the bottom of the hinges in from the cabinet edge. By using this to position each hinge as shown, all hinges will be in alignment. Drill pilot holes and secure the hinges with screws (see page 105 for more on installing hinges).

Mount doors. Now you're ready to mount the doors to the face frames. To make sure all the doors align, consider making a guide to support the doors so you can secure them to the cabinet. To make the guide, first center a door on an opening from top to bottom and measure the distance between the end of the door and the bottom of the face frame. Cut a strip of $^3/_4$" scrap to this measurement, and attach a piece of $^1/_4$" hardboard to the bottom of the strip so it extends out and creates a lip. Position the guide on the bottom rail of the cabinet so the lip catches on the front, and clamp it in place as shown (top right photo). Now you can rest the doors on the guide, center them in the opening, drill holes, and secure them.

Add new hardware. The final step is to add the new hardware. See pages 103–104 for more on drilling accurate mounting holes and installing hardware.

Adding Crown Molding

One of the best ways to add elegance to a kitchen is to attach crown molding to the wall cabinets. This can be done both on cabinets that leave a space between their tops and the ceiling, and on cabinets that go all the way up to the ceiling. Crown molding is especially useful with ceiling-height cabinets because it can conceal any gaps between the cabinet tops and the ceiling caused by an uneven ceiling.

You can attach crown molding manufactured from matching wood, as shown here. Another popular look is to use paint-grade molding (sold at most home centers), and paint the molding to match the accent colors used in the kitchen. As a general rule, choose molding that's around 3" to 4" wide for a standard 8-foot ceiling. Anything wider will appear out of scale.

Although attaching crown molding to cabinets is fairly straightforward, cutting the complex molding to wrap around the cabinets—especially in places that aren't 90-degree corners, such as around a corner cabinet—can be tricky. Fortunately, with the aid of a power miter saw, this can be done without too much head scratching.

ADDING A FLAT MOLDING

■ Because crown molding rests against a wall or cabinet at an angle, it has only two small flat sections that make contact. This makes it difficult to attach, since you need to hit a stud or joist for the nail to hold. One way to get around this is to first attach a flat molding. The flat molding is easy to attach to the wall, ceiling, or cabinet and provides a continuous nailing surface for the crown molding. In addition to providing a nailing surface, these moldings also offer a more pleasing profile.

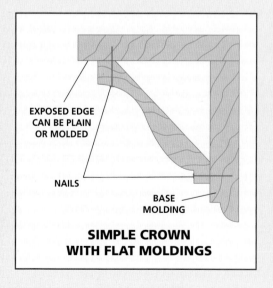

EXPOSED EDGE
CAN BE PLAIN
OR MOLDED

NAILS

BASE
MOLDING

**SIMPLE CROWN
WITH FLAT MOLDINGS**

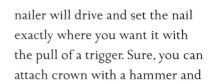

Reference line and strip. If you're installing crown molding to the tops of cabinets that don't go up to the ceiling (as shown here), start by using a long level to make reference lines on top of cabinets. To provide maximum nailing surface for the molding, locate the line about 1/4" up from the tops of the cabinet doors. If you're working alone, consider clamping a scrap of wood to the face frame to support the molding for nailing (inset at right).

Cut crown molding. And now for the tricky part: cutting crown molding to length. It's a good idea to practice your first few cuts on scrap until you get the hang of it. The safest way to hold crown molding for accurate cuts is to clamp a scrap to the base of a miter saw, as shown below, to hold the molding at the proper angle. When joining together two lengths of crown, cut the ends at opposing 45-degree miters to create an almost invisible "scarf" joint (inset below). When possible, cut miters first and then trim the molding to length, always erring on the long side.

Attach molding. The best way to attach crown molding is with an air-powered finish nailer (you can find these at most rental centers). A finish nailer will drive and set the nail exactly where you want it with the pull of a trigger. Sure, you can attach crown with a hammer and nails, but the chances of dinging the molding are extremely high. Also, since the finish nailer is used one-handed, your other hand is free to hold the molding—not so with a hammer and nails. If you notice small gaps at any of the mitered joints, you can close the gaps by "burnishing" the joint with the shank of a screwdriver—press firmly to crush the wood fibers and fill in the gap (inset below).

Optimizing Storage Space

Why is it that no matter how large a kitchen is, there never seems to be enough storage space? Too much stuff, possibly, but there's often space that's unused or not optimized for maximum storage. Of these spaces, the ones that are most commonly overlooked are under cabinets and sinks, inside the cabinets themselves, and in corners. Here's where under-cabinet storage racks, under-sink trays, pull-out bins, and appliance garages can help.

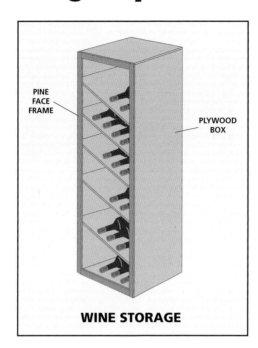

PINE FACE FRAME

PLYWOOD BOX

WINE STORAGE

Under-cabinet storage. There are numerous storage products available that can maximize the space under your cabinets. Wine racks, pull-down spice racks, cookbook racks, stereo systems…all of these are designed to attach to the bottom of your wall cabinets. Note: Another nifty storage idea for wine is the simple box with slanted shelves shown at left.

SINK TRAY

■ The area behind the false front of your sink cabinet can be used for storage by adding tilt-out sink trays. They're inexpensive and easy to install. Begin by removing the false fronts from the sink cabinet; then locate and drill pilot holes for the screws that hold the sink tray in place.

Attach bin to front. Drive the tray-mounting screws partway into the pilot holes you just drilled in the back face of the false front. Set the tray in place and snug up the screws so they're friction-tight. This will let you lift out the tray for cleaning.

Attach hinges to face frame. Next, locate the pilot holes for the hinges on the inside edges of the face frame, using the template provided. Drill pilot holes and secure the loose half of the hinge to the cabinet frame.

Attach hinges to false front. Use the template provided by the manufacturer to locate the tilt-out hinges that attach to the back side of the false front. Drill pilot holes and secure the hinges with the screws provided.

ADDING AN APPLIANCE GARAGE

■ Appliance garages fit between the countertop and bottom of the wall cabinet and feature a pull-down door to reduce countertop clutter. Small appliances (like toasters and blenders) are stored within until needed (see the corner appliance garage featured in the kitchen on page 98).

An appliance garage kit (far right photo) consists of a door unit, a pair of sides to match your cabinets, and an instruction sheet. The door unit has a pair of grooved tracks that guide a wood tambour up and down. A spring on top rolls the tambour much like the mechanism on a window shade.

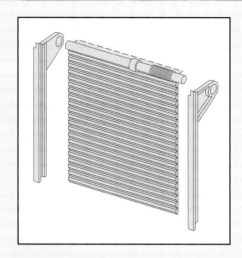

Assemble unit. In most cases, you'll need to assemble the sides of the door unit. See the manufacturer's instructions for assembly information.

Secure unit. Next, follow the manufacturer's instructions on how to attach the garage to the wall and cabinets. Some models have plastic tabs inside the appliance garage that are screwed to the wall.

Pull-out units. Bins and shelves that pull out of a cabinet not only are back savers, but they also maximize the space by making everything within accessible. Depending on the configuration, these can be used for storing dry goods, pots and pans—even recycling and garbage.

Attach pull-out mechanism. Follow the manufacturer's instructions

to locate and install the pull-out mechanism. This may be a single unit (as shown) or separate glides that attach to the inside faces of the cabinet.

Add shelves or bins. Next, install any support pieces (such as wire racks) and then insert the bins or attach the shelves to the shelf glides previously installed.

Adding a Kitchen Island

A kitchen island is a real problem solver. It provides space for storage, space for seating and, most importantly, work space. You may have struggled trying to shoehorn a small table and chairs into the kitchen; although this does provide seating, it doesn't help with storage and usually interferes with work flow. A tidier solution is an island with an overhanging top. Just find base cabinets that match your existing cabinets at a home center or unpainted-furniture store. Mix and match units to create your perfect island: You may want all-drawer units or all-door units—or a combination of the two.

Regardless of the configuration, the backs and sides of the cabinets need to be covered with finished panels. Most cabinet manufacturers make these, but you can cut matching plywood panels yourself. If you're building the island up from several units, start by attaching them to each other. Position the cabinets side by side with the face frames flush, and clamp them together. Then secure the units with drywall screws around the top, bottom, and front edges of the cabinet.

Position on floor and mark. The island attaches to the floor via a set of 2×4 cleats. Start by positioning the island where you want it and check for necessary clearances: walkways, appliance and cabinet doors, and between the overhang and the nearest wall where the stools will go. Then draw a line around the base.

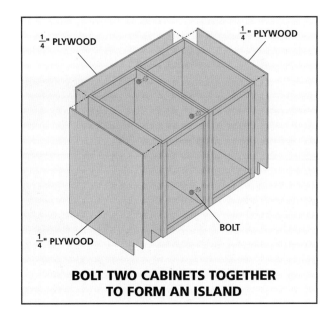

¼" PLYWOOD

¼" PLYWOOD

¼" PLYWOOD

BOLT

BOLT TWO CABINETS TOGETHER TO FORM AN ISLAND

Secure island to floor.

Cut a pair of cleats to fit under the cabinet, one cleat for each side of the cabinet (not the front and back). Position the cleats on the floor, taking into account the thickness of the cabinet walls. Then secure the cleats with 3" drywall or deck screws. Lift the island up and over the cleats; level it as necessary with shims, and then screw the island to the cleats as shown (these screws will be covered later with trim).

Add trim.

It's easiest to complete any trim before you attach the top. Cut a back from matching plywood (and sides, if necessary) and attach it with

glue and brads. Cover the exposed plywood edges at the corners with a strip of molding held in place with tape until the glue dries (bottom left inset).

Add the top.

Whether you choose to cover the top with plastic laminate or tile, you'll want a sturdy substrate, especially if there's an overhang for seating. Use a double layer of $^3/_4$" plywood. Measure your island (keeping in mind the desired overhang, if any), and cut two pieces 3" wider and longer than this to create a $1^1/_2$" overhang on each side. The top attaches to the island by inside corner clips. For a tiled countertop, refer to pages 121–125. If you prefer a plastic laminate top, refer to the directions on pages 118–120.

Removing Old Cabinets

TOOLS

- Pry bar and putty knife
- Drill or screwdriver
- Shop-made cabinet brace
- Adjustable wrench

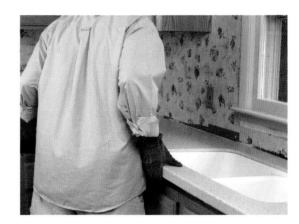

To someone who's never ripped out a set of kitchen cabinets, it might seem like a simple job. You just pry them off the wall, right? Wrong. That's the last thing you want to do because cabinets are screwed to the wall studs. To properly remove cabinets, you have to reverse-engineer the installation process. That is, you need to know how they were installed—check out pages 98–102 for a typical installation.

Remove trim and countertop. Since the trim was the last thing installed, it's the first thing to go in demolition. Use a pry bar and stiff-blade putty knife to protect walls, and remove all trim, including backsplashes. Then disconnect the sink and faucet and remove all the countertop fasteners. Lift off the countertop and set it aside for reuse or disposal.

Remove doors and drawers. Next, to make it easier to remove and carry the cabinets, take the time to remove all the doors and drawers to lighten the load. If you'll be reusing the cabinets for storage

somewhere else (they make great shop cabinets), label the parts with masking tape before you remove them so you can easily reassemble them later.

Disconnect plumbing. Before you can remove the base units, you may need to disconnect plumbing lines; it all depends on how they were routed through the cabinet. If necessary, shut off the water and remove the shutoff valves if the piping comes up through the base of the cabinet. This will allow you to lift the cabinet up and out. Waste lines will need to be disconnected and temporarily plugged with a rag to prevent sewer gas from leaking into your house.

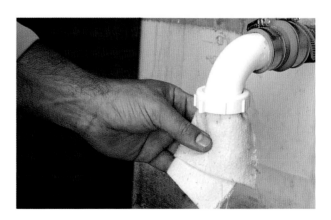

Release cabinets. Depending on how the base cabinets were installed, you may have to remove the cove base or base trim. This is necessary only if you need to expose screws driven through the base of the cabinet into the floor to secure it. Otherwise, locate and remove the screws in the backs of the cabinets that secure them to the wall.

Remove base cabinets. You should now be able to lift and pull the base cabinets away from the wall. If you encounter resistance, you've probably missed a mounting screw. If so, locate and remove the screw or screws and try again—in older cabinets, these may be hard to find, as installers often covered screw heads with putty to make them less visible.

Remove wall units. The wall units can now be removed. Before you remove your first screw, make a simple brace from scraps of 2×4 and plywood to support the cabinets temporarily. Wedge the brace under a cabinet, and start by removing the screws in the face frame securing the cabinets together. Then locate and remove the screws in the back of the cabinet that secure it to the wall. Lift the cabinet off the brace and set it aside. Repeat for the remaining wall units.

Installing New Cabinets

The ultimate makeover project for a kitchen is replacing kitchen cabinets. No other project will have as profound an impact as new cabinets. And, no other project is as costly. Easily half the cost of the average kitchen remodel job is for the cabinets.

The best way to protect this investment is to have the cabinets installed by a professional. Besides the cost issue, installing cabinets is a fine art: The cabinets must be shoehorned into an exact space with little or no clearance. In essence, the job is a large, complicated built-in.

This is not to say that cabinets can't be installed by a homeowner…they can be. It's just that the skills and the tools required are many. First, you need to be knowledgeable about cabinet construction so that you can take one apart and modify it if necessary (something an installer does in about half of all jobs). Secondly, you need finely tuned woodworking skills, including scribing, cutting, planing and fitting parts together, mitering and coping molding—even expertise in finishing is also needed. Add to that the required basic and advanced framing skills, and it's easy to see why using a pro makes sense. The following pages illustrate a typical installation handled by a 25-year veteran cabinet installer and his assistant.

Unpack and check parts.

Cabinets are often shipped directly to your door from the manufacturer. When the shipment arrives, check each package carefully for signs of damage before accepting shipment. If you find damage, open the package with the delivery person still present and note any broken items on the bill of lading, and then contact the distributor or manufacturer for a replacement (bottom left photo). Do not uncrate the cabinets unless the installer asks you to—the packaging often has the part numbers the installer needs to identify which cabinet goes where.

Find high point of floor. A successful cabinet installation begins with identifying the highest point on the floor. This is the starting point for all layout and measurement. The installer will use a bubble or laser level to find this and will mark the high point on the walls. He'll then measure up the height of the cabinets and draw a line around the perimeter of the room.

Level corner cabinet. In most cases, an installer will start with a corner cabinet and work his way out in both directions. Since this cabinet will serve as the foundation for the rest of the installation, the installer will spend quite a bit of time shimming the cabinet bottom until it's both level and plumb.

Add second cabinet and level. With the corner cabinet level and plumb, cabinets can be added to the sides of the corner cabinet. Each cabinet is shimmed as necessary to level the top of the cabinet from side to side and from front to back; the installer also checks to make sure the cabinet front is plumb. Filler strips are added as needed (see the sidebar on page 102).

Secure cabinets. At this point, the installer will begin screwing the cabinets together and to the back wall. Pilot holes are drilled though the edges of the face frames, and long screws are driven in to attach the cabinets. Then the screws are driven through the back of the cabinet into wall studs located during the layout process (right inset). All of the standard base cabinets are added in turn.

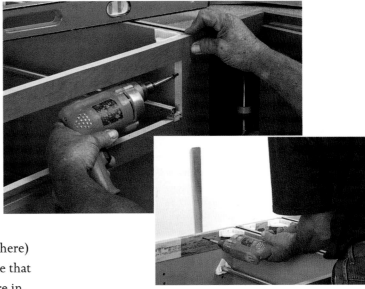

Install tall cabinets. Specialty cabinets (such as the tall wall-oven cabinet shown here) are installed next. A pantry is another tall piece that is usually installed after all the base cabinets are in. These heavy units are jockeyed carefully into position, made level and plumb, and secured to the adjoining cabinet. In some cases, the base of the cabinet is secured to the floor for added insurance (inset below).

Attach end panels. For better appearance, end panels are installed next to appliances (both built-in and freestanding models) to cover the sides. The installer will clamp one in position temporarily and then secure it to the adjacent cabinet with screws. Often, he'll drive a screw through the base of the end panel and into the floor to prevent the panel from twisting.

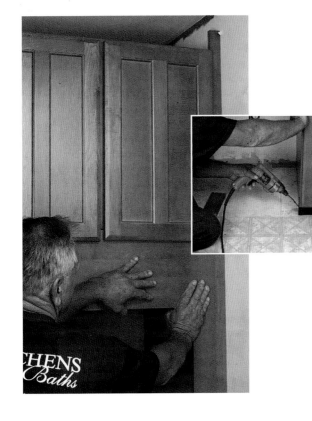

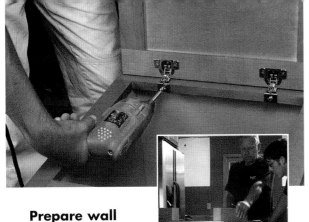

to lighten the load and install blocking on top of the cabinets to make installing crown molding easier (left inset).

Prepare wall cabinets. Once all the base cabinets are in, the installer will tackle the wall cabinets. Note that some installers start with wall cabinets and then install the base cabinets: They feel they have better access to the wall cabinets this way. But this isn't possible with ceiling-height cabinets and crown molding if you want consistent spacing between the countertop and wall cabinets; it's best to install the base units first. Installers will often temporarily remove doors

Install wall cabinets. To get consistent spacing between the countertop and the wall cabinets, the installer here supports the wall cabinet on spacer blocks he cut from scrap wood. These spacers help support the cabinet so it can be leveled and secured to the wall. Adjoining cabinets are installed in a similar manner, always using the blocks for spacing.

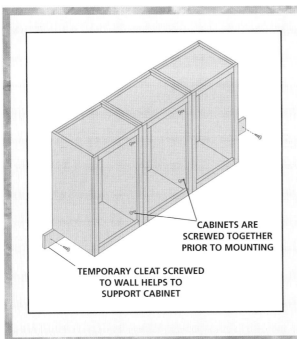

CABINETS ARE SCREWED TOGETHER PRIOR TO MOUNTING

TEMPORARY CLEAT SCREWED TO WALL HELPS TO SUPPORT CABINET

ALTERNATE INSTALLATION METHOD

■ Instead of installing cabinets one at a time, some installers level and plumb sections of cabinets in groups and fasten them together. Then they temporarily attach a cleat to the wall directly below the line where the wall cabinets will be installed. With the help of an assistant or two, the assembled unit is lifted up onto the cleat. Then the cabinet is checked for level one more time and secured to the wall studs. When strong backs are available, this method can speed up installation.

Nail trim base to wall cabinets. If crown molding is to be installed, it may be a single piece, or made up from multiple pieces (as shown here). The installer will start by measuring, cutting, and attaching the trim base to the tops of the cabinets. Odds are that he'll use a finish nailer for this.

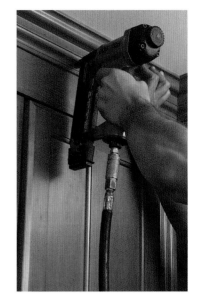

Attach crown. Finally, the installer will attach the crown molding itself. If you like magic shows, this is a great one to watch. The effortlessness with which a pro installs crown molding will appear to be magic. Complex angles, wrap-arounds… no problem. When all the trim is in place, the installer will re-install the doors and then add the cabinet hardware, along with any specialty items such as pullout bins, appliance garages, etc.

FILLER STRIPS

■ Since cabinets come in standard sizes and kitchens do not, there will inevitably be gaps between cabinets and walls— sometimes even between cabinets, because of the configuration. Here's where filler strips come in. Filler strips are just planks of wood finished to match your cabinets. An installer will measure, sometimes scribe, and cut a strip to perfectly fill the gap. Once cut, the strip is attached with screws to the closest cabinet to the wall. When done right, the cabinets will look like they were custom-built on site to fit from wall to wall.

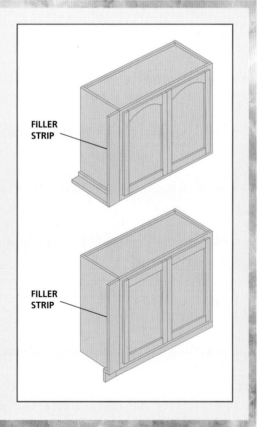

FILLER STRIP

FILLER STRIP

Cabinet Hardware

Although it may seem like a small detail, the hardware you choose for your kitchen cabinets can have a large effect on the overall design. Everything from drawer knobs and pulls to the door hinges can play a part in how the kitchen is perceived. The hardware will also have an impact on how easy it is for the cook to work—just think about how many times you open and close drawers and doors in preparing a single meal.

Cabinet hardware is a very personal thing. Some folks like knobs, other prefer

pulls. But whatever you end up choosing will look good and work well only if it's installed properly. This means that each piece must be carefully positioned and precisely installed. That last thing you want is a screw popping out of a cabinet front from an overly long hinge screw. That's why it's so important to make sure the hardware you buy is compatible with your cabinetry.

All hinges are not created equal. The hinge has to match the type of door: partial overlay, full overlay, inset, etc. If you're in doubt, check with a design professional or the manufacturer of the cabinet or hardware. They'll be able to resolve any incompatibility issues.

Pulls can also cause headaches; the distance between each side isn't standard. You'll find 3", $3^1/4$", $3^1/2$", and so on. Knobs, with their single screw, tend to simplify installation. Also, if you're purchasing knobs or pulls for drawers with false fronts (see Four-Sided Drawers on page 88), you'll need to pick up some longer screws. Most home centers have specialty screws that feature snap-off threads that can be customized to fit your drawers (left photo).

Drilling holes for knobs and pulls. There are a couple of things to consider when you drill holes in cabinet doors and drawers for new hardware. First, position is critical, so use a drilling guide (see the sidebar below). Second, if you don't back up the part that you're drilling into, the drill bit will splinter the back of the part as it exits the hole. To prevent this from happening, temporarily clamp a

scrap of wood to the back of the door or drawer. This "backer board" will support the wood fibers of the door or drawer. Yes, it will splinter if you drill completely through it, but that's the point: Better a splintered piece of scrap than your cabinetry. Note the splintered backer board in the photo—that's what the back of your door or drawer would look like without it.

SHOP-MADE DRILLING GUIDE

■ Accurate placement of cabinet hardware is something you notice only when a knob, hinge, or pull is out of alignment. Then, it sticks out like the proverbial sore thumb. To prevent this, it's worth the time and effort to make a simple drilling guide. The guide is just a piece of $1/4$" plywood or hardboard with cleats on both faces to serve as lips to automatically position the guide for drilling.

Once you've decided on placement for the hardware, measure the distance up from the bottom and offset from the adjacent edge; transfer these

measurements to the guide (see the illustration at left). Then drill the desired-size mounting hole in the guide at this location.

To use it, you position the guide on the corner of a door or drawer so the cleats butt up against the edges of the part (see the photo above). Then simply drill through the hole in the guide (make sure to use a backer board), and all your hardware will be perfectly aligned.

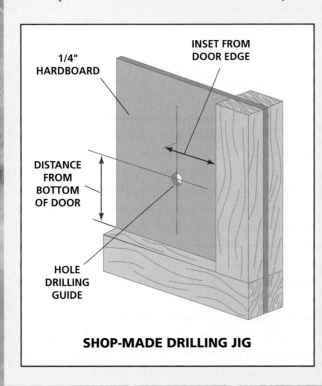

1/4" HARDBOARD

INSET FROM DOOR EDGE

DISTANCE FROM BOTTOM OF DOOR

HOLE DRILLING GUIDE

SHOP-MADE DRILLING JIG

32mm HINGES

■ Some cabinetry—particularly frameless cabinets—feature 32mm hinges. These specialty hinges have the advantage of being totally adjustable. That is, you can adjust a door up and down, side to side, and in and out after the door is installed. One half of this two-part hinge attaches to the face frame or inside face of the cabinet. The other fits in a round recess drilled into the door. Four screws adjust the door's position as shown below.

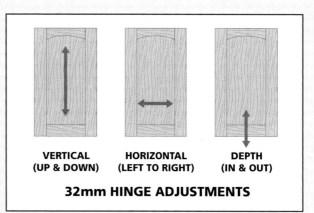

| VERTICAL (UP & DOWN) | HORIZONTAL (LEFT TO RIGHT) | DEPTH (IN & OUT) |

32mm HINGE ADJUSTMENTS

VERTICAL   **HORIZONTAL**   **DEPTH**

Installing hinges.

Probably the most challenging cabinet hardware to install is hinges. That's because there are so many things to go wrong: The hinge itself can twist out of alignment as it's secured to either the door or face frame, the door can twist out of alignment as it's being secured to the face frame, or the door can be improperly centered on the opening. Fortunately, each of these can be prevented. Use the guide shown on page 89 to center and align the door or doors on the opening and prevent it from twisting out of alignment.

To prevent the hinges from twisting as they're secured to a door or face frame, use a self-centering bit (often referred to by the trade name Vix bit). A self-centering bit is a totally reliable way to install a hinge without the usual skewing and misalignment. The "magic" of this bit is an inner and outer sleeve that spins around a twist bit. When the tip of the self-centering bit is inserted in a hinge hole and depressed, an inner sleeve retracts up into the outer sleeve. This positions the twist bit so it can drill a perfectly centered hole for the hinge screw.

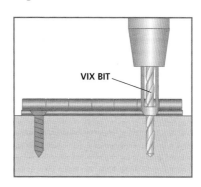

VIX BIT

6

KITCHEN COUNTERTOPS

We set hot pans on them. We use them as cutting boards. We spill all kinds of food on them, scour them with rough cleansers, and still expect them to look great. Poor countertops. They take even more abuse than kitchen floors, and that's why durability is priority number one here.

Of the many choices in materials today, only two are do-it-yourself-friendly: plastic laminate and ceramic tile. Older laminate countertops in good condition can be re-laminated. Or you can replace worn-out tops with precut laminated countertop, available at home centers. Ceramic tile? It's messy, yes, but easy to install, especially on the flat horizontal of a counter surface.

The "glamour" countertops—solid-surface acrylic, granite, quartz—must be left to the pros. They're very expensive, and in many cases the warranty is voided if a noncertified installer does the job. We'll cover the basics here so that you'll know what to expect if you have one of these deluxe materials installed.

Relaminating a Countertop

TOOLS

- Power sander
- Drill or biscuit joiner
- Circular or saber saw
- Laminate trimmer
- Laminate roller

Why relaminate a countertop? For the same reason you'd put a fresh coat of paint or new wallpaper on the walls of your kitchen. As long as the underlying structure is sound, you don't need to tear down the walls for a new look. The same thing applies to a countertop. If your existing countertop is in good shape but the pattern or color is worn or dated, why not "paint" it with a new layer of plastic laminate?

That said, relaminating isn't for every kitchen. It can be done only on countertops that have a flat backsplash, or no backsplash. You can't relaminate a post-formed countertop—the kind where the laminate flows up and over a curved backsplash in a single piece (see page 113 for an example of this). Bending laminate around small-radius corners like this can be done only by the large machines at countertop factories.

Also, the existing laminate must be securely bonded to the substrate (the underlying base), typically plywood or particleboard. If the old adhesive has failed and there are spots where the laminate has lifted or is loose, consider replacing the countertop (see pages 113–117). Bonding new laminate to old laminate that's loose will only cause headaches in the future.

There are a number of options for edging the existing countertop. You can apply a narrow strip of laminate to the front edge, but odds are this will not hold up over time. A more durable solution is to attach a wood strip to the front edge and then laminate over this. Profiling this edge with a router leaves a strong, attractive edge.

Prepare old countertop. The first step in relaminating a countertop is to prepare the old surface. For the adhesive to bond well with the old laminate, it must be scored or roughened. This gives the adhesive something to "bite" into. A belt sander fitted with a coarse belt (60- to 80-grit) will make short work of this. Take care not to round the corners over at the front edge.

Add edging. To add wood edging to the countertop, cut a strip of hardwood (preferably oak or maple) to match the thickness and length of the countertop. The strip is best secured to the front edge with dowels or wood biscuits. These provide shear strength if someone presses down on the strip (such as when kids try to pull themselves up on the counter). Apply glue to the dowels or biscuits and press the strip in place (inset at right). You could use nails or screws instead, but they're not as strong and will show.

Apply new laminate. With the edging in place, you can lay the laminate. Cut the laminate to size and apply at least two generous coats of contact cement to each surface. Use only solvent-based contact cement for this. Although water-based doesn't smell as bad, it will not bond the laminates together as well. When the cement has dried to the touch, position the laminate on dowels or strips of wood placed on the counter to prevent premature adhesion. Pull out the dowels, working from the center toward the ends, and press the new laminate in place with a laminate roller (inset). (Note the blue tape "X"—this identifies the sink opening so you don't press down here and fracture the laminate.)

and run the bit around the perimeter of the opening to cut out the laminate.

Rout decorative edge. All that's left is to rout a decorative profile on the front edge. This can be as simple as the small chamfer shown here, or as fancy as a Roman ogee. Note that when you profile this edge, you'll be cutting into both  the laminate and the edging strip. This leaves a clean edge with no gaps. Mask off the laminate, and seal the wood strip by applying a couple of coats of polyurethane.

Cut out sink opening. If the countertop you're relaminating has an opening for a sink, the next step is to remove the laminate that covers the opening. To do this, first drill a starter $1/2$"-diameter hole for a flush-trim router bit. Then insert the bit fitted in a laminate trimmer or router into this hole,

CREATING A PERFECT JOINT

■ Relaminating a single length of countertop is fairly straightforward. Things get complicated, however, when the countertop wraps around a corner in an L or U shape. This means you'll need to join pieces of laminate together—the tricky part is creating a seam that doesn't show. Here's a nifty way to make an "invisible" seam.

Cut the pieces to width and then clamp them together as shown between a pair of scrap wood guides. Then simply

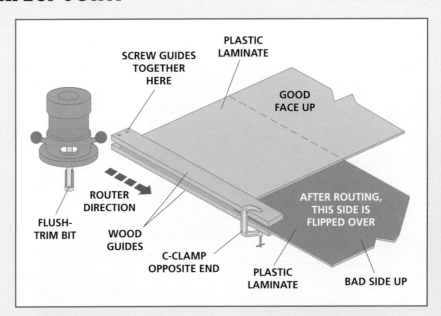

SCREW GUIDES TOGETHER HERE

PLASTIC LAMINATE

GOOD FACE UP

ROUTER DIRECTION

FLUSH-TRIM BIT

WOOD GUIDES

C-CLAMP OPPOSITE END

AFTER ROUTING, THIS SIDE IS FLIPPED OVER

PLASTIC LAMINATE

BAD SIDE UP

run a router or laminate trimmer fitted with a flush-trim bit along the guides. Routing the edges at the same time like this creates matching mating surfaces that, when brought together, will create a perfect seam.

Removing an Old Countertop

If you're planning on a new countertop as part of your makeover, the old countertop will have to go. How you remove it depends on whether or not it was site-built. As described on page 26, the countertop on site-built cabinets is attached to the cabinets from above; all other countertops are attached from below. Countertops attached from below are simple to remove (see page 112). What makes site-built countertops a challenge is that after the top is secured, the laminate is applied—and this covers the fasteners. To get to these, you'll likely need to remove portions of the laminate (see below).

SITE-BUILT

Pry off backsplash. The first step to remove a site-built countertop is to pry off the backsplash (if there is one). Protect the wall by inserting a wide-blade putty knife between the wall and the backsplash. Use a pry bar to pull the backsplash out. It probably will be nailed every 16" into the wall studs.

Remove laminate. If the countertop is secured with nails, you may be able to pry it off without removing any laminate. If screws were used, you'll need to remove portions of laminate to expose them so they can be removed. If you try to pry off the countertop without unscrewing these screws, you'll cause severe damage to the underlying cabinet frames. To remove laminate, first cut the edge with a utility knife. Then inject lacquer thinner to dissolve the contact cement (top inset).

Lift off countertop. Now you can peel off the laminate to expose the fasteners. Stubborn nails can be removed with a cat's paw (inset below). When all the fasteners are out, carefully lift off the countertop and set it aside for disposal.

POST-FORMED

Most standard countertops, including the post-formed laminate countertop shown here, attach to the cabinets with screws from underneath. The screws may pass through the cabinet frame and up into the countertop, or they pass through plastic or wood corner braces and into the top.

Release countertop. To remove a post-formed counter-top, start by releasing the top. Remove the screws that hold the

top in place. Then run a utility knife between the back of the backsplash and the wall. This will cut through any caulk that provided a seal. When caulk hardens over time, it can create quite a bond. If you don't cut it, you run the risk of damaging the wall as the countertop is pulled away.

Lift off countertop. If your countertop consists of one or more sections spliced together, remove the hardware holding them together (see the sidebar below). Then all that's left is to lift off the countertop and set it aside for disposal. As you remove the top, take care to pull it toward you and away from the wall to prevent wall damage.

DEALING WITH SPLICED SECTIONS

■ Post-formed countertops are often spliced together from short sections to go around a corner. The ends are mitered to create a neat joint. The sections are held together with special fasteners that fit into grooves routed into the underside of each section. When removing a countertop with sections like this, it's easier to knock the countertop apart so you can work with shorter, lighter sections. To pop the sections apart, loosen the splice hardware from below and remove them. Then, from above, give the mitered joint a sharp rap or two with a hammer. This will break the glue bond that helped hold the sections together. Now the parts can be easily separated and set aside for disposal.

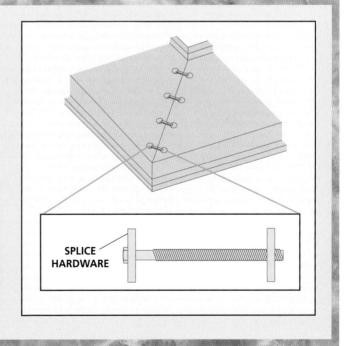

SPLICE HARDWARE

Installing a Post-Formed Countertop

TOOLS

- Circular saw
- Saber saw (optional)
- Belt sander
- Compass
- Hammer
- Adjustable wrench
- Tape measure and level
- Household iron
- Screwdriver
- Caulk gun

There's a good reason why post-formed laminate countertops are so popular in kitchens. They're durable, extremely stain-resistant, and inexpensive. Not only that, you can find precut lengths in a variety of colors and patterns at most home centers. Post-formed laminate countertops are made with a backsplash attached: The manufacturer bends the laminate around a hot post to form the curve. To make it even more convenient to install, sections are available with left- or right-mitered ends and with sink openings partially cut; all you need do is complete the cut and remove the waste. You'll also find matching end caps (see page 116), splice hardware (see page 112), and build-up kits for counters where dishwashers are installed (see page 114).

As long as your cabinets are the same lengths as the sections that are available, installation is a breeze. But in a less-than-perfect world, you'll probably need to trim the sections to length. And here's where things get tricky. Because of the way a post-formed countertop is made—particularly the backsplash—it's difficult to make a clean, straight cut. Fortunately, you can make a simple cutting guide that will let you cut the sections to length with precision (see page 115 for more on this).

If you're not interested in the hassle of cutting or trimming countertop to length, you can order custom-cut lengths at most home centers. The only drawback is that you'll have to pay for the service.

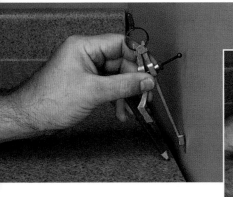

run the point against the wall. The pencil will scribe the unevenness of the wall onto the top so you can trim the countertop to match.

Cut to length. If you need to cut a section to length, use the cutting guide shown on page 115. If you just need to trim the end a little, remove as much waste as possible with a saber saw and then use a belt sander held on its side to sand up to the line.

Scribe ends to fit against wall. Even when you use countertop sections that are cut to length, you'll most likely need to trim the ends to fit flat against your walls. That's because few if any walls are really flat. To fit an end perfectly against a wall, start by "scribing" the end. Scribing transfers the irregularities of a wall onto the countertop; it can be done with a compass or a scrap of wood with a hole in it for a pencil (inset above). Just open the compass until the legs span the largest gap, and

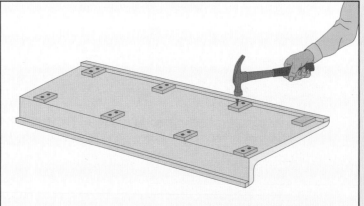

BUILD-UPS FOR DISHWASHERS

■ If the cabinets on which you're installing the countertop house a dishwasher, you'll need to add build-up blocks to allow clearance for the appliance. These raise the countertop up so the door of the dishwasher doesn't catch on the front lip. Build-up kits are available wherever you purchased your countertop, but you can save some money by cutting your own from scraps of plywood or particleboard. They're $1/2$" thick and roughly $1^1/2$" × 3". Place the countertop upside down on a flat surface and secure the blocks with glue and nails every 12" or so around the front and back edges of the countertop.

CUTTING GUIDE FOR POST-FORMED COUNTERTOP

■ The secret to cutting post-formed laminate countertop to length with precision is to use a cutting guide. The shop-made guide shown here is made of scraps of $^3/_4$" plywood and $^1/_4$" hardboard. The plywood is screwed together in the shape of an L to form the base that your circular saw rides on. The hardboard attaches to the plywood to create a lip to guide the saw for a perfect cut.

To make the guide, start by measuring the width of your saw base and add 4" to this. Cut two strips of $^3/_4$" plywood to this width: one 24" long, the other $2^7/_8$" long. Screw the two pieces together as shown in the illustration below. Then cut two strips of $^1/_4$" hardboard 4" wide, and 24" long and 5" long. Attach these to the plywood base as shown.

Now clamp the guide onto a worktable or bench so the plywood side overhangs the bench. With the base of your saw against the hardboard, cut through the plywood on the long and short sides. This trims away any excess and creates an edge at the exact position of the saw blade; this can then be used to align the jig when cutting the countertop.

Clamp to countertop. Place the countertop upside down on a work surface, and measure and mark the cutoff point. Then place the guide and slide it over until the cut edge of the guide aligns with the cutoff mark. Secure the guide to the countertop with clamps, making sure the back of the guide butts up against the back of the backsplash.

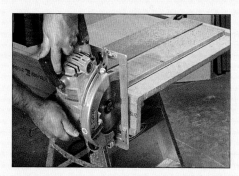

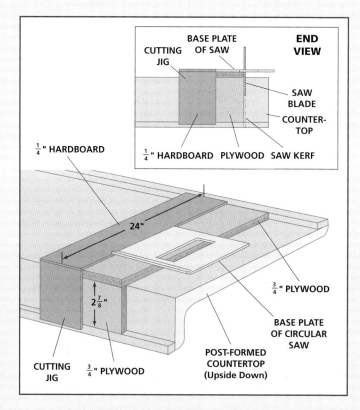

END VIEW

CUTTING JIG · BASE PLATE OF SAW · SAW BLADE · COUNTER-TOP · $^1/_4$" HARDBOARD · PLYWOOD · SAW KERF

$^1/_4$" HARDBOARD · 24" · $^3/_4$" PLYWOOD · BASE PLATE OF CIRCULAR SAW · $2^7/_8$" · POST-FORMED COUNTERTOP (Upside Down) · CUTTING JIG · $^3/_4$" PLYWOOD

Cut to length. With the guide in place, start cutting the countertop to length by cutting through the backsplash as shown. Then make the long cut. The only trick here is to go slow and keep the saw's base in constant contact with the hardboard strips. When done, soften the sharp edges of the laminate with sandpaper or a smooth-cut mill file.

Prepare for end caps. Where the ends of a post-formed countertop will be visible, they're covered with "end caps." These are strips of laminate precut to match the shape of the ends; they're coated on the reverse side with hot-melt glue, and you attach them to the ends by softening the glue with an electric iron. Before you attach the end caps, you'll need to build up the countertop to form a gluing surface for the end caps. Most end-cap kits contain the necessary filler strips; they're attached with glue and nails as shown.

Apply end caps. Now you can attach the end caps. Place the end cap on the end of the countertop and run a hot iron over the laminate until the glue melts. Keep steady pressure on the end cap as you move the iron back and forth to heat up the entire strip. Once the glue cools down and the end cap is firmly attached, you may need to trim it a bit, as they're often made slightly oversized. A laminate trimmer fitted with a flush-trim bit will make short work of this. Finally, soften the edges of the laminate with sandpaper or a smooth-cut mill file.

CORNER CABINET SUPPORT

■ If your new countertop is going over older cabinets, you may need to provide additional support for the countertop in the corners. Before cabinet manufacturers started making the nifty corner cabinets we have today, a corner cabinet was made by pulling one cabinet out from the wall and then attaching the adjacent cabinet 90 degrees to it. This left a space in the corner which offered no support for the corner of the countertop. If your cabinets are like this, you should screw a cleat to the wall as shown to fully support the corner of the countertop.

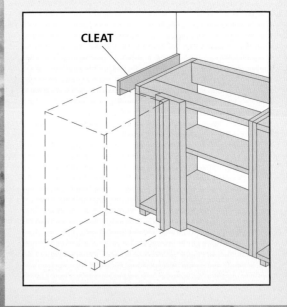

CLEAT

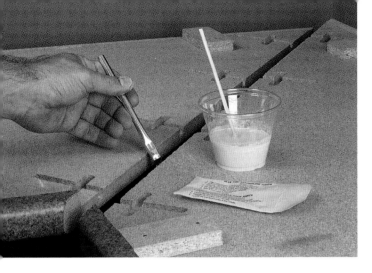

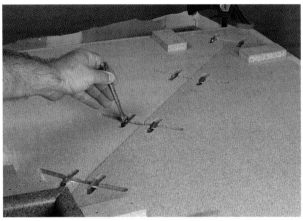

Join sections together. With the end caps and build-ups in place, you can join any sections together prior to placing them on the countertop. Start by roughly positioning sections upside down on the cabinets. Then pull them apart at the seams and apply glue to the ends of the miters. Push the sections back together and install the splice connectors. Match the rounded front nose edges of the countertop and tighten the nearest connector. Do the same for the backsplash, then flip the countertop right side up and position it on the cabinets. Make sure the tops of adjoining sections are flush with each other, and then fully tighten the splice connectors.

Level countertop and secure to cabinet. Once the countertop is in place, you can level and secure it. Insert shims between the underside of the countertop and the tops of the cabinet frames as necessary to bring it level. Then secure the countertop to the cabinets by driving screws up through the cabinet frame or through corner braces, whichever is applicable.

Caulk at backsplash. The final and hugely important installation step is to apply a bead of caulk where the backsplash meets the wall. Here again, you'll likely have gaps since most walls aren't perfectly flat. The caulk fills the gaps and provides a watertight seal that will protect not only your walls, but also the easily water-damaged particleboard substrate of your countertop.

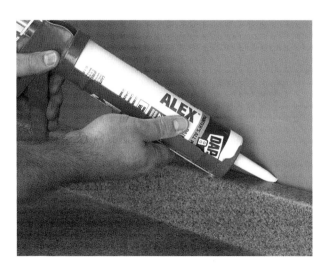

Adding a Snack Bar

With a little creativity, you can shoehorn a snack bar or eating surface into almost any kitchen. In the kitchen shown here, we took advantage of a wall partition and simply attached the snack bar directly to the top of the partition. Another way to get an eating surface in the kitchen is to add a wall-mounted snack bar (see the illustration at right).

Both versions use the same construction methods. A double layer of plywood or MDF (medium-density fiberboard) is wrapped with hardwood edging and covered with plastic laminate. The beauty of this arrangement is that it's so easy to customize the shape of the top to fit your needs. Notice that in the version shown here we mitered one corner to provide wider access into the kitchen (see the top view on page 52). The wall-mount version just needs a pair of support brackets and a cleat for attaching to the wall.

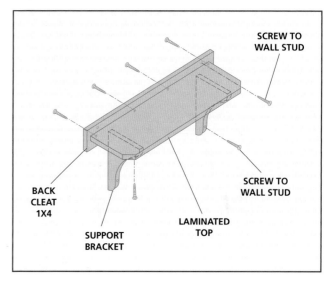

SCREW TO WALL STUD

SCREW TO WALL STUD

BACK CLEAT 1X4

SUPPORT BRACKET

LAMINATED TOP

Prepare substrate. To make a snack bar, start by screwing together two pieces of ³/₄"-thick plywood or MDF. Next you can add the edging. As with the edging for the relaminated countertop on page 108, this edging is best attached with dowels or biscuits. Lay out and drill holes for dowels or cut slots for biscuits. Since you'll need to make a matching set in each edging strip, temporarily clamp the strips to the top and mark them both at once. Then drill holes for dowels or cut slots for biscuits with a biscuit joiner.

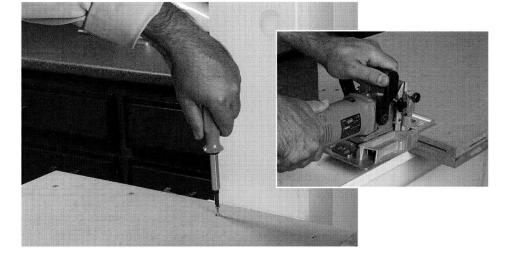

Apply edging. Now you can attach the edging. Apply glue to the dowels or biscuits and a generous bead to both the edging and the plywood or MDF. Press the edging in place and apply clamps to bring the pieces up tight against each other.

Secure to partition. If your snack bar will rest on a partition, now is the time to attach it; this way, the laminate will hide the fasteners. For wall-mount units, it may be easier to laminate the top and then attach it to the wall cleat and supports.

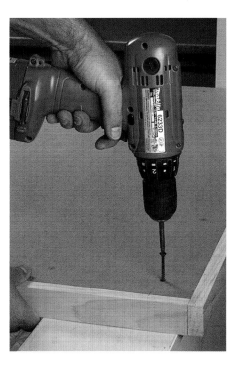

Trim laminate. Now you can trim the laminate to the exact shape of the top. The best tool for this is a laminate trimmer with a flush-trim bit (bottom left photo). Just run the trimmer around the perimeter, keeping the bearing of the bit in contact with the edging.

Finish edges. All that's left is to rout a decorative profile on the edge and apply a finish to the edging. We went with a simple chamfer here, but you can dress up the edge with a round-over or other decorative profile. Sand the edging and brush on a couple of coats of paint or clear finish; just make sure to first mask off the laminate.

Apply laminate. To apply the laminate, start by cutting it an inch or two larger than the top. Then roll on two coats of contact cement to the laminate and the plywood or MDF top. When dry to the touch, place strips of scrap wood or dowels on the top to prevent the adhesive from making contact until the laminate is in perfect position. Then, working from the center out, pull out a dowel or scrap and press down. Work toward the ends like this until the laminate is in place. Then press the two surfaces together with a laminate roller.

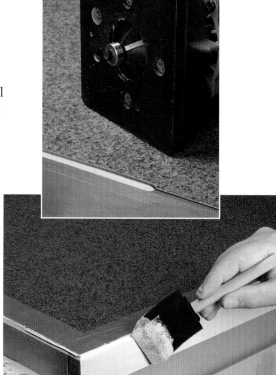

Tiling a Countertop

TOOLS

- Tape measure and framing square
- Tile cutter and nippers
- Notched trowel and putty knife
- Grout float
- Electric drill and screwdriver
- Staple gun
- Hammer
- Dead-blow hammer or rubber mallet

Ceramic tiles offer a richness of texture that no other countertop surface can match. Add to this the superb depth of color and the varying patterns, shapes, and sizes of tile, and you can see why a tiled countertop can add a touch of elegance, even luxury, to even the smallest kitchen. But what really makes tile an excellent choice for a countertop makeover is that it's inexpensive, readily available, and easy to install. Sure,

it's messier and more time-consuming than other countertop installations, but if you take it one step at a time, each task is simple and fairly easy—even if you've never laid tile before.

There is one drawback to tile: the grout lines. Grout is a putty-like substance that fills in the spaces between the tiles. If left unsealed, the grout is easily stained by food spills. But this can be avoided by applying grout sealer. The secret to grout longevity is to regularly reapply the sealer; see the manufacturer's instructions on how often this should be done.

With proper preparation, you can cover just about any surface with tile. Tiling over plastic laminate is possible as long as the laminate is securely bonded to the countertop. Don't be afraid to mix and match countertop surfaces; a tiled island or wall-mounted counter (at left) can provide a nice contrast to solid-surface or laminate countertops. (An example of this is the tiled island in the kitchen on page 54 that features Corian countertops.)

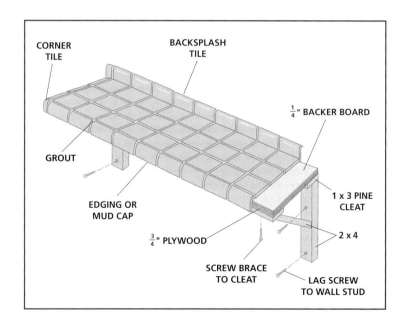

CORNER TILE

BACKSPLASH TILE

$\frac{1}{4}$" BACKER BOARD

GROUT

EDGING OR MUD CAP

1 x 3 PINE CLEAT

$\frac{3}{4}$" PLYWOOD

2 x 4

SCREW BRACE TO CLEAT

LAG SCREW TO WALL STUD

Prepare surface. If you're tiling a new surface where the substrate is plywood or MDF, the first step is to add a layer of backer board to create a foundation for the tile. The backer board is secured to the substrate with thin-set mortar and screws. To prevent the wet mortar from damaging the substrate, the first step is to cover the substrate with a layer of 3- to 4-mil plastic. Staple the plastic under the edges of the countertop if possible, and then trowel on the mortar.

Attach backer board. Following the manufacturer's instructions, cut the backer board to size and also cut strips to attach to the edge of the countertop. Attach the backer board and edge strips with cement screws; these special screws should be available where you purchased

your backer board. They're stout, galvanized screws that have small fins under the heads to cut a countersink in the backer board as they're driven in. This way, the head of the screw ends up flush with the surface.

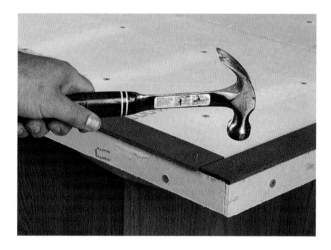

Install guide strips. If you plan to edge the countertop with bullnose tiles as shown on page 124, the next step is to temporarily attach strips of wood to the countertop to serve as guides for the tiles. Mark a line along the edge of the countertop to allow for the width of the bullnose tiles. Align the guide strip with this line and temporarily attach it to the countertop with nails. For wood edging where the tiles will be flush with the front edge of the countertop, temporarily attach a strip of wood to the front edge of the countertop to serve as a guide.

Position full tiles. Apply mortar to the backer board with the appropriate-sized notched trowel, working in a 2- to 3-foot-square area. Begin laying tiles by working out from the corner. The tiles shown here have built-in tabs for spacing the tiles; other tiles may require rubber spacers to set the gaps between the tiles. Press a tile firmly into the mortar, wiggling it slightly as you press down to set it into the mortar. Continue filling in tiles on each side of the first tile; use spacers if necessary to create even gaps for the grout that will be applied later.

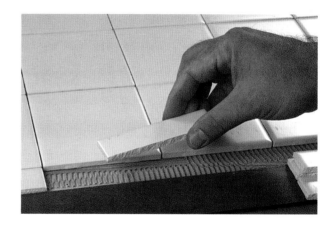

Position partial tiles. Once all the full tiles are in place, go back and cut tiles as necessary to fill in any spaces. After the tiles are placed, they can be set. Setting tiles presses them firmly into the mortar and also levels the surface. A simple way to do this is to give each tile a gentle rap with a dead-blow hammer or rubber-faced mallet (top inset).

TILING AROUND A SINK

■ The most complicated part of tiling a kitchen countertop is tiling around a sink. The tricky part is positioning the tiles so you end up with evenly spaced tiles on both sides of the opening. Here's how to handle this: Begin by placing a row of tiles along the front edge of the sink. Then measure the tiles at each end to the center of the opening. Adjust the tiles as necessary until the excess on each end is the same. Then mark the end of the tiles and use a framing square to extend this line to the backsplash. This line is the starting point for the entire countertop.

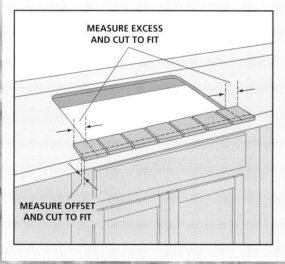

MEASURE EXCESS AND CUT TO FIT

MEASURE OFFSET AND CUT TO FIT

Add edging tiles. When all the full and partial tiles have been set, you can attend to the edging tiles. First remove the temporary guides. Then apply mortar to the tiles—this is less messy than applying it to the backer board. Just slather on some mortar on both of the inside faces of the tile and press the tile in place. For end caps (see the sidebar at right), apply mortar to the tile back and press it in place. (Attaching a back-splash is similar; see page 125 for options.)

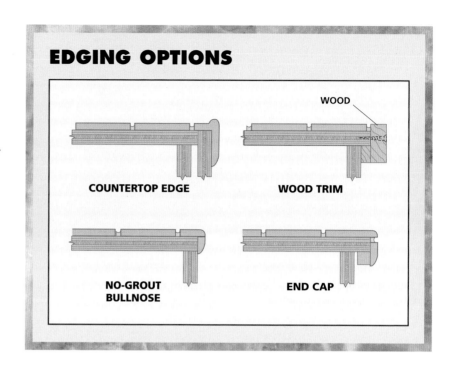

EDGING OPTIONS

COUNTERTOP EDGE

WOOD TRIM

WOOD

NO-GROUT BULLNOSE

END CAP

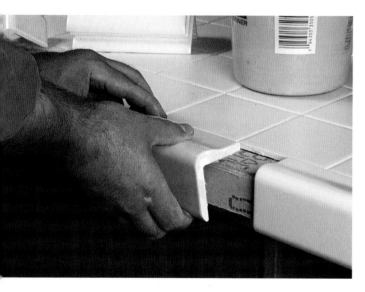

Apply grout. Let the mortar dry overnight, and then mix up enough grout to fill in the gaps between the tiles. Apply the grout with a grout float diagonally to the surface to force the grout between the tiles. To remove the excess, hold the float at about a 45-degree angle and scrape the surface, taking care not to pull the grout out from between the tiles (photo at right).

Remove excess grout. When the grout becomes firm, wipe off any excess with a slightly damp sponge. Here again, it's important to work gently because the sponge can and will pull the damp grout right out of the joint. Work slowly and keep the sponge just barely damp, rinsing it in clean water frequently. Next, allow the grout to dry to a haze and then wipe off any remaining grout with a clean, soft cloth.

Seal tiles. You'll have to wait 2 to 4 weeks to complete your tiling job. That's the length of time most sealer manufacturers recommend before applying a sealer to the grout. Check the label of your grout sealer to find out how long you should wait. This waiting time allows all the water in the grout to evaporate. If you apply sealer prematurely, it will trap water inside, which will eventually create mold.

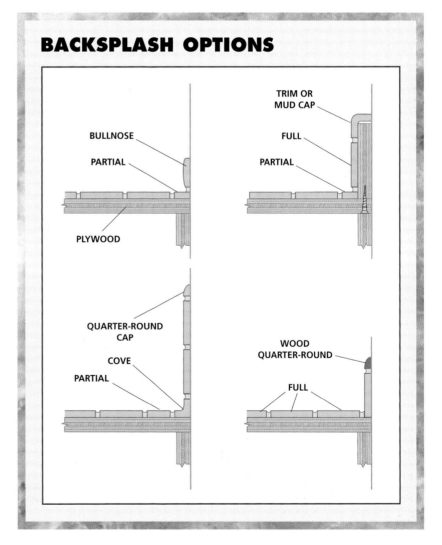

BACKSPLASH OPTIONS

BULLNOSE

PARTIAL

PLYWOOD

TRIM OR MUD CAP

FULL

PARTIAL

QUARTER-ROUND CAP

COVE

PARTIAL

WOOD QUARTER-ROUND

FULL

Solid-Surface Countertops

ACRYLIC COUNTERTOP

When you're ready to step up to today's generation of countertops, consider solid-surface. Solid-surface countertops are an advanced blend of natural materials and pure acrylic polymers. Besides coming in a huge array of colors and patterns, what makes a solid-surface countertop truly unique is that it's solid all the way through. This is different from laminate or tile countertops, where cutting produces a raw, exposed edge of plywood or particleboard. When you cut into solid-surface material, you get solid surface. And this means you can cut it, rout it, carve it, add decorative inlays—even sandblast it—without restriction. If you want to inlay a complex pattern on the edge, or rout drainage grooves into the surface near the sink, there's no problem.

In addition to the flexibility of design and construction that solid-surface materials offer, they are nonporous, resist stains well, and are easy to clean.

TEMPLATING

■ The first step in fabricating a solid-surface countertop is templating. Your local authorized dealer will send out a certified installer to make a template of your new countertop. This is typically done with heavy-duty corrugated cardboard and thin strips of wood glued to the edges for support. Once the template is made, it goes back to the factory, where it serves as a template to shape the actual countertop.

Attach template. The installer starts by temporarily attaching the cardboard strips to your cabinet frame with hot-melt glue. Then narrow wood strips are glued around the perimeter to create a stiff edge.

Lay out and dimension. The installer then measures and marks the template. He'll lay out the location of the sink, the ends of the countertop, and any other necessary cutouts (such as an island cooktop). Armed with this template and the pattern for any openings, he returns to the factory, where the top is made.

And because of its solid composition, the surface can be periodically renewed if necessary.

The most common of the solid-surface materials is DuPont Corian®. Corian is manufactured into sheets and sinks. The sheets are precut into specific lengths at the factory (the most common size is 145" × 30" × 1/2") and then shipped to trained professionals, who fabricate and install the product. This is the only drawback to a solid-surface material: It can be purchased only through a distributor and shaped and installed only by a certified fabricator/installer. That's because cutting, routing, and joining solid-surface materials is somewhat hazardous—it's best left to a professional.

Trim to fit back wall.

Even with the most careful templating, odds are that one or more of the back or side edges will need to be fine-tuned for a perfect fit. In most cases, the installers will handle this on the spot by removing the offending material with a belt sander held on edge. For large variations, they may have to return the top to the factory, but they'll do everything to prevent this once the countertop has been delivered.

Add support.

As the typical sheet of solid-surface material is only 1/2" thick, the edges are built of two layers and then profiled—this is usually done at the factory. To help support the countertop once it's installed, the fabricator will often glue strips of the material at strategic points to strengthen the top. Alternatively, some installers will build a simple wood frame to serve as a support and secure this directly to the cabinets.

Drill faucet holes.

Once the countertop has been fitted and is in place, the installers will usually drill the faucet holes. This is done with an electric drill fitted with a standard hole saw. In some cases, the holes will be drilled at the factory, but most fabricators prefer to have this done on-site with the faucet in hand so they can ensure that the holes are the correct diameter and spaced correctly apart. If the sink being installed is an under-mount, it will be attached now.

Install countertop. The final placement of the countertop is sort of a wrestling match between the installers and the countertop. This is especially true with an L- or U-shaped countertop that must be wedged in between cabinets. The weight and awkwardness of the countertop adds to the drama. What makes it so difficult is that the edges of the countertop can easily damage the walls and cabinets. Here's where the experience of the installers will be truly evident.

Seal with caulk. The final step is to seal the back edge of the countertop with silicone caulk. The installers should do this whether or not a backsplash is to be installed. Sealing the joint between the countertop and the wall is added insurance against moisture damage. If desired, you can have them fabricate and install a solid-surface backsplash, or add a tile backsplash yourself (see page 125 and pages 142–145 for more on tile backsplash options).

Secure countertop. When the installers are pleased with the fit, the sink is in place, and the faucet holes have been drilled, they'll secure the countertop to the cabinet. In most cases this means propping the front edge of the countertop up temporarily and applying a few dollops of silicone caulk to the front top edge of the cabinets. Since a solid-surface top is heavy, this is all it takes to secure it. The weight of the top itself helps hold it in place.

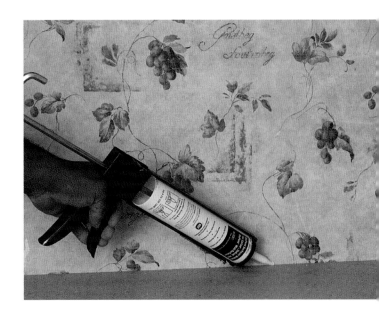

Quartz Countertop

For the ultimate in solid-surface countertops, consider quartz. DuPont manufactures a solid-surface material called Zodiaq. It's composed mostly of quartz (93%), which makes it exceptionally tough—quartz has a hardness of 7 on a scale of 10 (only diamonds rate a 10). A quartz countertop is dense and nonporous and requires no sealing. In addition to being strong and durable, quartz is heat-, scratch-, and stain-resistant. It's easy to maintain and offers unusual depth, clarity, and radiance. The ultra-smooth surface will maintain its lustrous gloss for many years without any sealants or waxes. And, it will not promote the growth of mold, mildew, or bacteria.

Like Corian, Zodiaq must be purchased through a distributor, who can set you up with a certified fabricator/installer. Slabs of Zodiaq come in one size (52" × 118") and two thicknesses ($^3/_4$"- and $1^1/_8$"-thick). Because this stuff is basically rock, it's extremely heavy: A $^3/_4$"-thick slab weighs over 700 pounds—another good reason to use professionals. It also requires diamond-impregnated tools for cutting and shaping—not something the average homeowner has lying around the house. Special adhesives are also needed to join sections together, along with a rather space-age-looking vacuum press that pulls the joint together (see the sidebar on page 131 for more on this).

Secure the countertop. As with the other solid-surface countertops, a quartz countertop is secured to the cabinets with silicone caulk. Because quartz is less flexible than a polymer countertop, the installer will also apply a bead of caulk along the front edge to seal any gaps between the tops of the cabinets and the underside of the countertop.

Seal the sink. Because quartz is solid all the way through, like its polymer cousin, it's well suited for under-mount sinks. The sinks can be held in place with clips that thread into inserts glued into the underside of the countertop around the perimeter of the sink opening. Alternatively, a frame can be built to support the sink under the opening. In either case, as the countertop is readied for final placement, the installer will run a generous bead of silicone around the lip of the sink to create a water-tight seal.

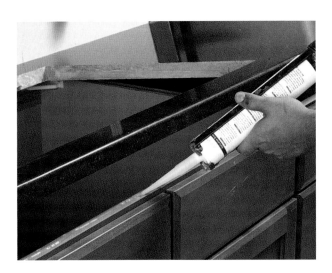

CUTTING QUARTZ

■ What makes a quartz countertop so tough also makes it difficult to cut and shape. The tools for this have to be heavy-duty, and all the bits and blades must be impregnated with diamonds. In addition to this, the ultrafine dust that's created

Cut openings as needed. Since the cooktop that was being installed in the peninsula portion of the high-end kitchen (see page 178) consists of three separate pieces, the fabricator decided it'd be best to cut the opening at the site with the appliances at hand.

Drill faucet holes. The faucet holes were also drilled at the site to ensure correct diameter and spacing. Note the masking tape applied to the top. It's used to mark the location of the holes and helps protect the glossy surface from being scratched.

from cutting or drilling will become airborne and quickly coat anything nearby. That's why the installers will ask to borrow your garden hose if they need to make a cut. They'll use the hose to drizzle water onto the countertop. This not only greatly reduces dust, but also helps keep the bit or blade cool. Whenever possible, all cuts should be made at the factory.

SEAMING QUARTZ

■ Unlike polymer solid-surface countertops, whose sections are virtually fused together with special adhesives to create invisible seams, the seams of a quartz countertop are more visible. That's because they're basically epoxied together. The epoxy is usually a two-part catalyzed mixture that sets up quickly.

Mix adhesive. To make the seam as invisible as possible, the installer will mix color into the adhesive so it closely matches the quartz countertop. Because quartz has varying shades, it's difficult to color-match. But if the sections were machined as precisely as they should have been, there will be little if any gap and this should not be an issue.

Applying glue to seams. Once the adhesive has been color-matched to the countertop, the installer will slather the epoxy mixture on the ends of the sections to be joined. To prevent the adhesive from sticking to the underlying cabinetry, he'll temporarily raise one portion. This also makes it easier to apply the adhesive.

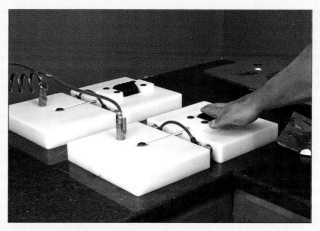

Pull seams together. All that's left is to join the sections. The installer uses a nifty vacuum clamp for this. The two halves of the clamp attach to the sections to be joined via suction. Then a switch is flipped and small motors rotate threaded shafts that pull the clamp halves together—and along with them, the countertop sections. When the sections are pulled tight, the installer will scrape off any excess adhesive with a putty knife. When dry, the seam is cleaned up with a scraper and should be hardly noticeable.

KITCHEN WALLS

7

Thanks to cabinets and appliances, the kitchen is one room where the wall space tends to be minimal. At the same time, this small space can have a big impact on the overall look and feel of the kitchen. Bold paint? Flowered wallpaper? Textured tiles? Your choices in colors, materials, and patterns can extend a decorating theme, provide a contrast, or pick up a tone in the countertop or cabinets.

There's more to this than just appearances, though. Naturally, you want your walls to be smooth and free of holes and bumps, so in this section we'll treat wall preparation. And some wall areas require special attention: You want to protect sections above countertops and behind the range from cooking grease, food stains, and water. Tile is a good choice here, and we'll look at selecting and installing this popular, durable material.

Wall Preparation

Ask professional painters what the secret to a flawless paint job is, and they'll tell you it's preparation. In fact, the preparation portion of any paint job should take longer than the time it takes to actually paint. Unfortunately, many homeowners skip these vital steps to save time, and end up disappointed. Wall prep isn't rocket science, but it does take time and patience. The first step is to clean the walls thoroughly. Scrubbing a wall lightly with a sponge or brush saturated with a cleaning solution of tri-sodium phosphate (TSP) will quickly strip off dirt and grime. Just make sure to rinse the wall completely with clean water when done. Then take the time to patch holes. How you do this will depend on the size of the hole.

Fill small holes. Small holes in drywall can often be patched by simply applying some putty, spackling paste, or drywall compound. Slightly larger holes are best covered with mesh tape or one of the convenient drywall patches sold at most home centers. These patches typically are thin squares of metal, covered with self-adhesive mesh tape. Just peel off the backing and place it over the hole; then apply a thin layer of joint compound to hide the patch.

Hide any stains.

After you've patched the holes in the wall, the next step is to hide any stains caused by water damage, food spills, etc. The quickest way to do this is with a couple of coats of stain blocker. You can find a few brands in the paint section of your local home center. These do an excellent job of hiding and sealing stains, and are available with either solvent- or water-based cleanup.

HIDING NAIL AND SCREW HOLES

■ If you've ever patched nail or screw holes with a patching compound, you may have been disappointed. That's because when the fastener is removed, it often damages the wall covering, leaving it torn and often protruding. No matter how carefully you apply putty or patching compound, the torn fibers won't lie down, and end up sticking out. Here's a nifty way to get around this: Place the head of a carriage bolt over the hole and give it a tap with a hammer. The round head of the bolt will create a smooth dimple in the surface that can then be filled—the hole will simply disappear.

PATCHING LARGE HOLES

■ Holes in drywall that are larger than an inch or so need a drywall patch. One of the simplest ways to patch a larger hole is with a drywall repair kit that uses special repair clips to secure the new patch to the wall. The clips support the new patch and then "disappear" once they've done their job to leave a smooth, clean wall.

Cut out damaged area. To use a drywall repair kit, start by cutting out the damaged area with a drywall saw or by taking a series of cuts with a utility knife.

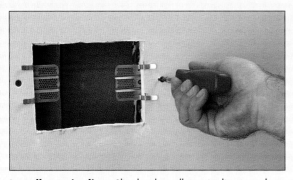

Install repair clips. Slip the drywall repair clips onto the edges of the damaged wall and screw them in place with the screws provided in the kit.

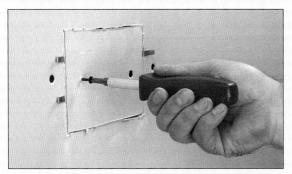

Install patch. Next, cut a patch from a scrap of drywall to fit in the hole you cut out, and attach the patch to the drywall clips by driving screws through the patch and into the clips.

Snap off exposed clips. Here's the beauty of this type of kit: Lever the exposed ends of the clips back and forth a few times, and they'll break off, leaving a smooth surface.

Hide patch seams. Now you can apply mesh tape over the seams and spread joint compound over the tape. Apply additional coats as needed, and then sand or sponge the seams smooth.

Painting Walls

TOOLS

- Paint tray and roller
- Trim pad
- Clean rags
- Foam brushes

One of the simplest ways to give a kitchen a quick makeover is with a fresh coat of paint. New paint can brighten the kitchen, change the mood, and even make it appear larger or smaller. Darker paints tend to close a space in, while lighter paints open a space up.

Latex paints are particularly well suited to kitchens, as they go on easy and clean up well. Since flat paints stain readily, better choices are eggshell, satin, or even semigloss paints.

Take the time to prepare the walls (see page 134) and make sure to cover the floor, the cabinets, and your appliances with drop cloths or old sheets. Tape the cloths or sheets with masking or duct tape to wrap around obstacles as needed. It's also a good idea to restrict access to the kitchen while you're painting. Even the tidiest painter will end up with some paint on the floor, and the last thing you want to discover when the job is done is a trail of footprints or paw prints leading out of the room.

Mask protected areas. Unlike simpler living spaces in the home, the walls of a kitchen require extensive masking. Not only do you need to mask around window and door trim, but you'll also spend considerable time masking off the kitchen cabinets. There are a couple of products that can speed up this process. One of these is combination tape and paper, like that shown in the photo. It comes in rolls with a self-adhesive that can be easily repositioned.

Apply primer.
Primer is another one of the steps that's often skipped to save time and money. But priming is an important step that helps ensure a good bond between the old surface and the new paint. It's formulated to make the old surface more "receptive" to the paint. Priming also seals damaged areas and hides stains. And if you have the primer tinted to match the paint, you may need only one coat of finish paint.

Paint walls with roller. Now all that's left is to fill in the large spaces with paint. A standard roller fitted with a disposable sleeve makes quick work of this. After you've rolled paint on a wall to cover it completely, go back and do what's called "striking off." Take your roller and begin at the top of the wall and roll it all the way to the bottom in a continuous stroke. This will remove any roller marks and leave you with a smooth, clean wall.

Paint around perimeter. After the walls have been primed, the next step is to paint around the perimeter of the room. A trim pad with rollers is a quick and efficient way to do this. These also work great for painting around the edges of the cabinets. The only trick to working with a trim pad is to keep the rollers free of paint. Check the rollers each time you load the pad, and remove any paint with a clean cloth.

Stripping Wallpaper

TOOLS

- Garden sprayer
- Perforating tool
- Bucket and sponge

If you've decided that the orange striped wallpaper in the kitchen has to go and it's time to paint, you first have to strip off the paper. How you strip it will depend on the wallpaper type and how it's glued to the wall. Many newer wallpapers are "strippable." That is, they can literally just be peeled off the walls. Older, pasted-on wallpapers can be removed by breaking down the glue. This is done by first perforating the wallpaper (see below) and then spraying on a removal solution. (Note: If you're planning on repapering the walls, you can paper over the old wallpaper as long as it's in good condition, is firmly bonded to the wall, and is relatively smooth.)

Perforate the wallpaper. You may or may not need to perforate the wallpaper before spraying on the solution. It depends on whether or not the paper is porous. To test this, wet the paper with a sponge. If it soaks in, you don't need to perforate. If it doesn't, the paper is coated and needs perforating. This entails punching tiny holes in the wallpaper with the aid of a perforating tool (often referred to by the brand name Paper Tiger). Just rub the tool along the wall as if you were washing it.

Spray on removal solution. Before you spray on the removal solution, cover cabinets and floors with drop cloths, seal electrical switches and receptacles with masking tape, and lay old towels at the base of the wall to collect any runoff. A garden sprayer works great to apply the solution. Follow the manufacturer's mixing instructions and fill the sprayer. Spray on generously to wet the paper. Wait 15 minutes, and spray on a second coat.

Peel off wallpaper. After waiting the recommended time, try to peel off the paper. If the solution has done its work, the paper will peel right off. If it doesn't, apply additional coats as needed to break down the glue. When all the paper is removed, wash the wall with clean water.

Wallpapering a Wall

Although applying wallpaper is more complicated than painting a kitchen, it does have a couple of advantages. First, if the old walls are in poor shape (lots of dings, dents, and stains), wallpaper can hide this multitude of sins. Second, the color, design, and texture palette that wallpaper offers is almost limitless. Wild or soothing patterns? Small geometrics or big floral prints? Textures that resemble bamboo, suede, watered silk…they're all yours for the choosing.

Granted, hanging wallpaper isn't quite as simple as painting, but it's fairly straightforward and easy to do—it just takes a bit longer. You'll still need to prepare the walls as you would for painting (see page 134), with the exception that you don't have to worry about hiding stains—the wallpaper will do that. Once the room is ready, set up a work station. A 2×4-foot piece of $^3/_4$" plywood on a set of saw-horses works well for this. Cover the plywood with a plastic drop cloth, and have plenty of towels on hand for spills.

Establish plumb line. Since most walls aren't straight, it's important to establish a plumb line for

laying the first strip of wallpaper. Begin at the least conspicuous corner of the room and press a 4-foot level up against the wall. Use a pencil to draw a plumb line. Then measure from the top to the bottom of the wall and cut a strip to length. For successive strips with a patterned paper, follow the manufacturer's measuring and cutting directions to ensure a pattern match.

Wet paper and book if necessary. Most prepasted wallpaper is re-rolled before wetting. This makes it easier to pull the paper out of the tray and take it directly to the wall for hanging (many of these require some "soak" time before they're hung). Other papers must be "booked" for a certain time to allow the paste to activate. This just means folding the strip back on itself so the paste sides come together. After waiting the specified time, you open the paper and apply it to the wall.

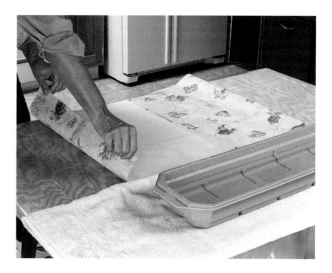

Hang paper. After you've waited for the paper to soak or book, grip the paper by the top edge and take it to the wall. Start at the ceiling and allow a 1" to 2" overlap. Align the strip with the pencil line you drew earlier, and press it into the wall with the palms of your hands.

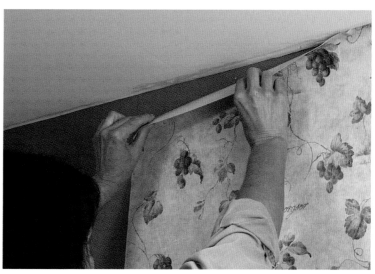

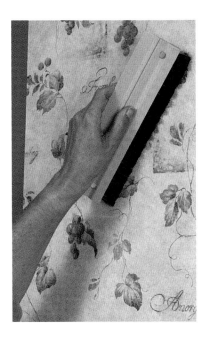

Smooth the strip.
With the strip in position, use a brush or a sponge to smooth it. Start at the top and use downward strokes, checking constantly to make sure the edge of the strip is still aligned with the pencil line.
Brush any air pockets out toward the edges. If you encounter a large wrinkle that can't be brushed out, peel off the strip and rehang it.

Trim paper to fit. To trim the paper at the ceiling, first press the paper into the corner with a wide-blade putty knife. Then peel it back, cut it with scissors at the fold you made with the knife,

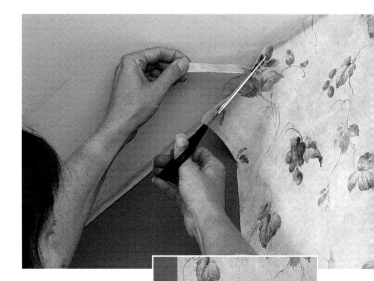

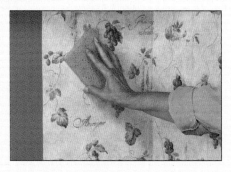

and press the paper back in place. To cut around electrical receptacles, first cut a small "x" with a utility knife. Then use scissors to cut out a rectangular area no larger than the box.

WORKING AROUND INSIDE CORNERS

■ When it's time to work around an inside corner, trim your first strip so it runs onto the adjacent wall $^{1}/_{2}$". Then hang a full-width strip on the adjacent wall, starting in the corner, taking care to

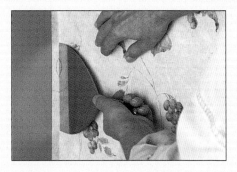

match the pattern. Although this method takes more time than simply allowing a wider strip to continue around the corner, it guarantees that the paper will fit snugly into the corner. This prevents air pockets from forming, which frequently occurs when a wider strip is allowed to continue onto the adjacent wall.

Single-Tile Backsplash

TOOLS

• Notched trowel
• Grout float
• Tile cutter
• Bucket and sponge
• Screwdriver

A single-tile backsplash is the perfect opportunity to add a splash of color to a kitchen while at the same time protecting the wall behind the countertop from food spills and water splashes. (Alternatively, you can tile the entire backsplash area; see page 144.) A tile backsplash also serves a couple of other functions. Even with the most careful scribing and cutting, there will likely be gaps between the countertop and the wall; tile will cover any gap. At the same time, a tile backsplash also provides a much-needed seal between the countertop and the wall and prevents water from seeping down the wall.

Although a little water trickling down the back wall may not seem like a big deal, it can become one. If you look closely at the photo of the original kitchen shown on pages 50–51, you can see a gap between the backsplash and the countertop. Over time, water that seeped through this gap managed to flow down the wall and into the flooring. Unfortunately, the subfloor was particleboard, which wicked the moisture into it as if it were a dry sponge. The end result was a spongy, possibly dangerous floor; the entire subfloor had to be removed and replaced.

That's why this seal is so important. Even after the backsplash is in place and everything is dry, you should go back and apply a bead of silicone caulk where the tile contacts the countertop. This is added insurance that you won't develop any moisture problems.

Affix backer board to wall. The type of wall covering behind your countertop will determine whether or not you need to first attach a strip of backer board. Some older homes have plastic laminate on the wall, and all you need do here is rough up the laminate with coarse sandpaper before applying thin-set mortar. If, instead, the wall is covered with drywall, you'll need to screw a strip of backer board to the wall to prevent the moisture in the mortar from seeping in and damaging the wall.

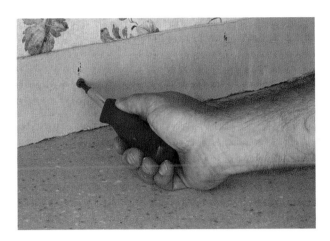

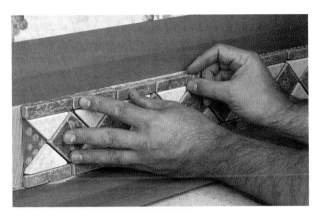

Apply mortar and set tile. With the backer board in place, mask off the wall area above it to keep mortar off the wall; mask off the countertop as well. Then trowel on some thin-set mortar; see the instructions on the mortar package for recommended notch size. Now you can position the tile by pressing it into the mortar.

Grout and trim. After the mortar has set, mix up sufficient grout and press it into the spaces between the tiles with a grout float. Squeegee off the excess with the float; when dry, wipe off the haze with a clean cloth. Note: Since the tile we used here didn't offer a bullnose, we painted strips of quarter-round trim to match and then secured this to the wall studs with brads (inset).

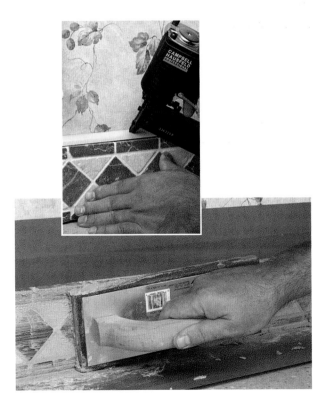

Full-Tile Backsplash

TOOLS

- Notched trowel
- Grout float
- Tile cutter
- Bucket and sponge
- Screwdriver

Ceramic tiles are one of the best all-around low-maintenance surfaces you can choose for a kitchen. No wonder they're the number one choice for protecting the walls behind a countertop. This area, appropriately named the "backsplash," takes a lot of punishment. But a tile backsplash can handle the day-to-day splattering: It's virtually immune to water and food spills, and can also take hard knocks from countertop appliances being pushed around.

A full-tile backsplash is a great way to add color and texture to your kitchen. Colorful mosaic tiles, hand-painted tiles, or glossy ivory tiles can all make a statement. If you've never worked with tile before, this is an excellent first project because the area is rather modest and there's little that can go wrong.

The biggest challenge to this job will probably be selecting the tile. As a general design rule, it's best to choose backsplash tiles that are 2" to 4" square, to keep everything in proportion. The small-est tiles (called mosaic tiles) come in 1" squares in sheets with nylon-reinforced backing. The advantage to these is that the spacing is preset: There's no need for spacers.

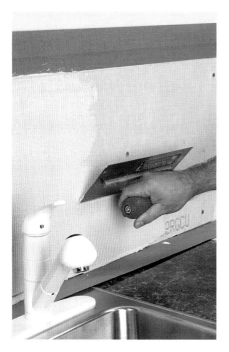

spacers between the tiles to create even gaps. Most ceramic wall tiles (like the ones shown here) have built-in tabs for spacing.

Add specialty tiles. Specialty tiles are available that can add visual interest to your backsplash. They can be understated, like the simple spiral shown here, or they can be a bold accent. You'll also find specialty tiles that are used to cap off the top row of tiles. These range from simple bullnoses to more elaborate "mud caps" that are simply pressed in place like the other tiles. When all the full tiles are in place, cut the partial tiles and set them. After you've applied grout and it's dry, remember to run a bead of silicone between the tile and countertop to create a seal.

Apply mortar to backer board. As mentioned in the single-tile backsplash section on page 142, the first step to tiling a backsplash is to secure backer board to the wall behind the countertop. After masking off the wall above the backer board and the countertop, trowel on thin-set mortar, using the recommended size notched trowel.

Position full tiles. The next step is to set the full tiles. Start at the bottom and work your way up, pressing tiles in place. If necessary, insert plastic

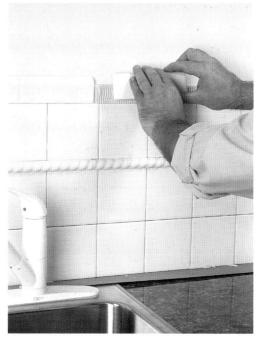

Painting or Replacing Window Trim

TOOLS

- Hammer
- Pry bar
- Stiff-blade putty knife
- Nail set
- Foam brush
- Miter box and saw

The trim in a kitchen is an important part of the overall design. It can help provide a transition between the walls and the cabinets, or it can serve as an accent. In either case, trim will likely either need painting or replacing in a makeover.

Mask off and paint. Trim that's in good condition can simply be repainted. Start by carefully masking off the wall and the glass. An easy way to get tape to fit squarely in a corner is to use a putty knife as a straightedge to tear the tape as shown below. Once the tape is in place, brush on one or two coats of quality trim paint.

Paint sash to match new trim. If you're replacing the trim with natural or stained wood, it won't match the painted sash of the window. Although this may not seem like a big deal, it will probably be highly noticeable. To prevent this, have your local paint store match some trim paint color to the new trim. Just bring in a sample of the trim and they'll mix paint to match it. Then once the old

trim is removed, mask off and paint the sash to match (top photo).

Attach new trim. Miter-cut new trim to fit around the window jamb. In most cases the trim is set back about $1/8$" from the jamb to create a reveal or shadow line. Use 3" casing nails to attach the outside edge of the trim to the studs and header that surround the window; secure the inside edge to the jamb with $1^1/2$" finish nails. To prevent the miters from opening over time, "lock-nail" the miters as shown in the drawing below.

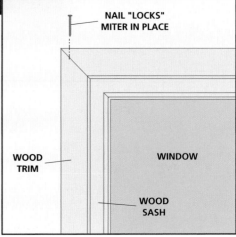

NAIL "LOCKS" MITER IN PLACE

WOOD TRIM

WINDOW

WOOD SASH

Removing a Wall or Partition

TOOLS

- Circular or reciprocating saw
- Hammer and sledge hammer
- Stud finder
- Crow bar or pry bar
- Stiff-blade putty knife
- Utility knife
- Screwdriver or drill
- Hydraulic jacks (optional)

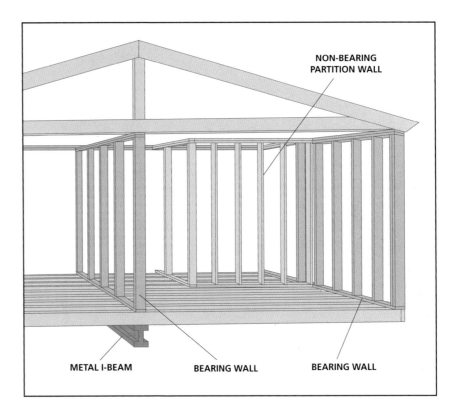

NON-BEARING PARTITION WALL

METAL I-BEAM   BEARING WALL   BEARING WALL

Before you remove a wall or partition wall in your home, you'll need to know if it's a load-bearing or non-load-bearing wall. A load-bearing wall helps support the weight of a house; a non-load-bearing wall doesn't. All the exterior walls that run perpendicular to the floor and ceiling joists in a structure are load-bearing walls because they support joists and rafters either at their ends or at their midspans (see the dark brown walls in the drawing). Also, any interior wall that's located directly above a girder or interior foundation wall is load-bearing.

Non-load-bearing walls, or partition walls, often have relaxed code requirements, such as wider stud spacing (24" vs. 16" on center) and smaller headers. The reason: They don't support any of the structure's weight (see the light brown walls in the drawing). If you're in doubt about a wall, contact your local building inspector for a definitive answer. Note: If you find you need to remove a load-bearing wall, get professional help, as you'll need to add support beams to compensate for the wall that's being removed. Calculating loads, and sizing headers and beams, is best left to a contractor.

The first thing to do to prepare for demolition work (which is what removing a wall is about, naturally) is to locate the framing in the wall or wall section to be removed. Use an electronic stud finder and mark the edges of the studs. Even the most sophisticated stud finder can occasionally be fooled by a plumbing or electrical line within the wall. It's best to verify stud positions by driving a finish nail through the wall on both sides of the stud. Also, if there are any receptacles or switches in the wall, identify which circuit breaker or fuse controls their power, and then shut off and tag the breaker or fuse and remove the cover plates.

Add support if necessary. Whenever a remodeling job requires that you remove a load-bearing wall or remove more than one stud in a load-bearing wall, you'll need to make temporary supports. The temporary supports bear the weight the wall normally would until a new support system can be installed (such as a new header or beam). The easiest way to support the wall is to build a T-shaped support structure that can be used for either parallel or perpendicular joists. The structure is pressed into place with hydraulic jacks.

between the two and gently pry the trim away from the wall. This takes a little extra time, but it will prevent damage to the trim. For situations where you know you won't be reusing the existing trim, you can remove it quickly with just a pry bar.

Remove drywall. To remove drywall, start by slicing through the taped joints at the seams and corners with a utility knife to keep from ripping the paper facing off the adjoining drywall surfaces. Then insert a pry bar and carefully pry back the drywall until you can slip your hands in to pull it away from the studs. Once you've got the framing totally exposed, here's your chance to confirm that the wall is what you suspected—either load- or non-load-bearing.

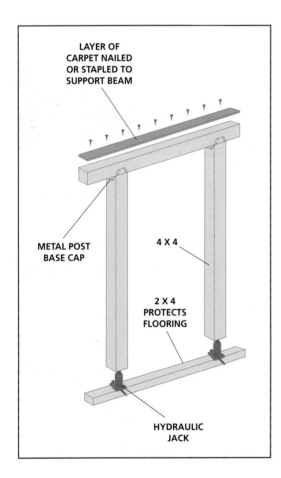

LAYER OF CARPET NAILED OR STAPLED TO SUPPORT BEAM

METAL POST BASE CAP

4 X 4

2 X 4 PROTECTS FLOORING

HYDRAULIC JACK

Remove baseboard and trim. If you plan to salvage the trim, it's best to remove it with two putty knives and a pry bar. Slip one putty knife against the wall, and insert a stiff-blade putty knife between it and the trim. Now insert a pry bar

Disconnect electrical/plumbing. Odds are there will be either electrical or plumbing lines in the wall you're working on. Make sure the power or water is shut off before you remove electrical and/or plumbing fixtures. Then you'll need to reroute the lines up into the attic or down into the crawl space or basement so they can be terminated properly.

Cut and remove studs. For a load-bearing wall, make sure that you build and install temporary supports for the wall you're removing. Some studs can be pulled off with a little persuasion from a hammer; others will need to be cut first. In either case, make sure to wear leather gloves and eye protection. To remove a cut stud, grip it, bend it back toward you, and lever it back and forth while twisting at the same time.

Fill sole plate gaps.

Whenever you remove a sole plate, you'll end up with a shallow 2×4-shaped channel that needs to be filled in—that's because flooring is always installed after a house is framed. The simplest way to fill this channel is to add strips of plywood cut to fit. Measure the depth of the channel, and mix and match thicknesses of plywood or hardboard; nail or screw the filler strips to the subfloor.

Adding a Wall

Typical wall construction. A typical 2-by wall consists of vertical wall studs that run between the sole plate attached to the subfloor and the top plate secured to the ceiling joists. Whenever an opening is made in the wall for a window or door, a horizontal framing member called a "header" is installed to assume the load of the wall studs that were removed. The header is supported by jack studs (also referred to as trimmer studs), which are attached to full-length wall studs, called king studs. The shorter studs that run between the header and the top plate or from the underside of the rough sill of a window to the sole plate are called cripple studs.

Install top and sole plate. To build a new wall in place, start by making the top and sole plate. Cut them to length and then butt them together so you can lay out the wall studs. Attach the sole plate to the floor, then use a plumb bob to align the top plate with the sole plate and attach the top plate to the ceiling joists; for a wall that's parallel to the ceiling joists, add blocking between the joists and screw the top plate to the blocking.

Cut and fit wall studs. With the top plate and sole plate in place, you can add the wall studs. Measure and cut one stud at a time: Chances are that the ceiling and floor are not par-

DOUBLE TOP PLATE

CRIPPLE STUD

KING STUD

HEADER

JACK STUD

COMMON STUD

HEADER

JACK STUD

KING STUD

SILL

COMMON STUD

SOLE PLATE

SOLE PLATE

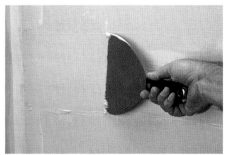
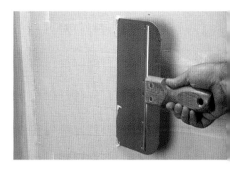

allel to each other. Cut the studs to fit snugly between the plates—a tight fit helps hold the stud in place for nailing. Toenail each of the studs to the top plate and sole plate. When the framing is complete, have your local building inspector check your work before applying drywall.

Attach drywall and tape joints. With the framing up, you can install drywall. Note that pros often install sheets horizontally, as shown here, as this makes taping easier. Drive screws or nails in so they sit just below the surface, but don't break through the paper covering. To conceal the joints between the sheets, apply drywall tape over the gaps. Do this by first spreading on a thin coat of joint compound and then pressing the tape into the compound with a wide-blade putty knife.

Create a smooth surface. When the tape coat is dry, apply a second coat with a wide drywall knife or putty knife. Cover the tape completely, and also all the impressions or "dimples" left by the screws or nails. When dry, use a stiff-blade putty knife to knock off any high spots. Then apply the next coat; use a wider drywall knife to feather the compound and create a smooth transition to the drywall. When this is completely dry, smooth the surface with a sanding screen or a drywall sponge.

INSIDE CORNERS AND OUTSIDE CORNERS

■ Creating smooth inside and outside corners with drywall can be a real challenge. Fortunately, there are tools and materials that make the job easier. For inside corners, consider investing in a corner tool (near right photo). The blade on this special applicator is thinner than a standard knife and is creased in the middle to form a 90-degree corner. As you press the tool into the corner and work it down the wall, the flexible sides conform to the adjacent wall and create a perfect inside corner.

Because outside corners are often subjected to a lot of abuse—especially in a kitchen—your best bet is to cover them with metal corner bead (far right photo). Corner bead is nailed or screwed to the corner of the wall. The point of the bead is rounded slightly to prevent dings and dents from showing. Once in place, joint compound is applied to conceal the bead and create a smooth transition to the drywall.

8

KITCHEN PLUMBING

O f all the plumbing fixtures in your home, the kitchen sink and faucet get used more than any others. So, naturally they need to be durable—but we never stop at practicality in our modern-day kitchens. Like every other element of your makeover, kitchen plumbing needs to look good, too, and manufacturers are happy to oblige. Gooseneck faucets, farmhouse sinks, finishes of brushed nickel or faux bronze… if it pours, sprays, or holds water, you can find it to fit your décor.

But water finds a way, so no matter what fixtures you choose, make sure they're properly installed to prevent damage from leaks. Installation can be a nasty business, because there's no elbow room under a sink, and you're often working flat on your back. But there are tricks to get around these troubles, and we'll look at the most effective ones here.

Materials

Choosing pipe. The pipe and fittings in your kitchen will be copper, galvanized, PVC (polyvinyl chloride), or a combination of these. The lines that supply hot and cold water are copper in newer homes, but may be CPVC (chlorinated polyvinyl chloride); older homes often use galvanized pipe and fittings. Drain, waste, and vent (DWV) pipe and fittings are typically PVC, but in older homes may be galvanized. Occasionally, larger copper fittings and pipe can also be used for small-diameter drainpipe. Exposed pipe and fittings are usually chrome-plated brass.

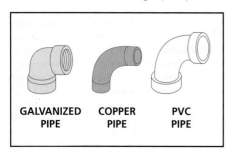

GALVANIZED PIPE   COPPER PIPE   PVC PIPE

Permanent vs. temporary fittings. The fittings that connect lengths of pipe can be permanent or temporary. Permanent fittings for copper are soldered or "sweated" together; with plastic pipe they're cemented together. Temporary fittings are often used in places where you know you'll want to be able to take things apart easily. These include supply lines and shutoff valves to fixtures that periodically need maintenance or replacement, such as faucets, dishwashers, and icemakers. The most common temporary fitting is a compression fitting, which has three parts: a fitting or body, a ferrule or compression ring, and a compression nut. The nut and ferrule slip over the pipe, which is inserted into the fitting. Tightening the nut compresses the ferrule into the fitting, creating a watertight joint.

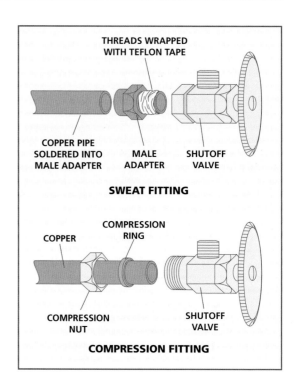

THREADS WRAPPED WITH TEFLON TAPE

COPPER PIPE SOLDERED INTO MALE ADAPTER   MALE ADAPTER   SHUTOFF VALVE

SWEAT FITTING

COPPER   COMPRESSION RING

COMPRESSION NUT   SHUTOFF VALVE

COMPRESSION FITTING

Flexible lines. Flexible supply and waste lines are a homeowner's dream. No specialty tools are required, just an adjustable wrench. Flexible supply lines run between shutoff valves and fixtures—usually in tight, cramped spaces. Flexible waste lines are often located next to their smaller cousins, except they connect sink drain lines to the waste stack. Most flexible waste lines use plastic compression fittings to make the connection.

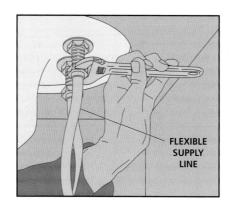

FLEXIBLE SUPPLY LINE

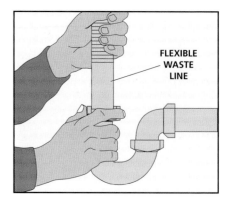

FLEXIBLE WASTE LINE

Removing an Old Sink

One of the most fundamental tasks in any kitchen makeover is removing the sink. Whether you're removing it to replace the countertop or the sink itself, the steps are straightforward.

Disconnect supply lines. To remove a sink, first turn off the water supply to the faucet. If the sink has shutoff valves, turn the knobs clockwise. If not, shut off the hot and cold water (the main valve and the water heater valve). Open the faucet to drain out any water in the pipes, and then use an adjustable wrench to loosen the coupling nuts that connect the supply lines to the faucet.

Disconnect waste line. If the drain hole in the new sink is located where the old drain was, you can take the easy way and loosen the slip nut on the drain tailpiece. Otherwise, you'll need to remove the trap and adjust its position to fit the new sink. With a bucket under the trap, use slip-joint pliers to loosen the slip nuts that connect the trap to the tailpiece. Then carefully remove the trap and empty it into the bucket.

Remove mounting clips. If the sink you're removing uses clips to secure the sink, the next step is to remove them. These clips hook onto a lip on the underside of the sink and pull the sink down tight against the countertop when the screws are tightened (see the drawing below). If possible, use a nutdriver or socket wrench to loosen the screws, as they are often corroded and will strip if a standard screwdriver is used.

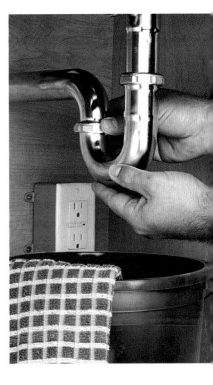

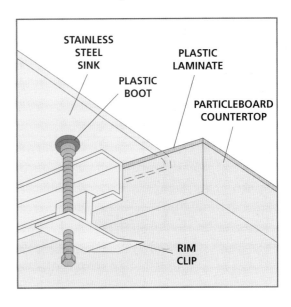

STAINLESS STEEL SINK

PLASTIC BOOT

PLASTIC LAMINATE

PARTICLEBOARD COUNTERTOP

RIM CLIP

originally applied under the sink's rim to create a seal will harden over time and behave as if it were cement. Run the blade of a plastic putty knife (to prevent scratching the counter-top) around the sink's rim to break the bond. If you skip this step and your countertop is plastic laminate, you run the risk of separating the laminate from the substrate.

Release and lift out sink. Before you can lift out the sink, you'll need to release it from the countertop. The plumber's putty or caulk that was

INSTALLING A SHUTOFF VALVE

■ Every fixture in your home should have its own shutoff valve. If this isn't the case, it's worth spending part of a weekend installing one for every fixture. When an emergency occurs or it's simply time to make a repair, you (and your family) will appreciate the fact that you can do the job without having to turn off the water for all, or part, of the house.

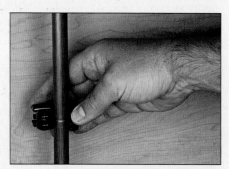

Cut lines. To install a shutoff valve, turn off the supply to the house (including the hot water line), drain the lines, and then cut the pipe where the valve is to be installed. To use a tubing cutter, open the cutter's jaws until it can be slipped over the pipe. Tighten the knob and rotate the tubing cutter around the pipe to begin cutting. Continue alternately tightening the knob and rotating the tubing cutter until you've cut through the pipe.

Compression-style valve. The quickest way to install a shutoff valve is to use a compression-type valve. Just slip the nut and com-pression ring over the pipe, press the valve onto the pipe, and tighten the nut.

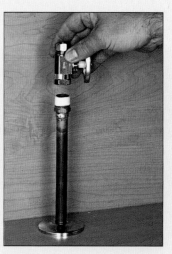

Sweat-type valve. These valves require more work but will provide a better seal. Start by sweating either a male or female transition fitting onto the pipe to match the valve. When cool, wrap a couple of turns of Teflon tape around the threads and tighten the valve onto the transition fitting.

Sink Openings

TOOLS

- Tape measure
- Electric drill
- Saber saw
- Foam brush

If you've replaced the countertop in your kitchen as part of the makeover, you'll need to cut out an opening for the sink. Although cutting the opening is easy, it's important to take your time locating the opening properly. (Note: Openings for solid-surface countertops need to be cut by a certified fabricator.)

Position template. Most sink manufacturers provide templates for openings. The trick to positioning the template is to start by centering it where you want it—in many homes, the kitchen sink is under a window. Start by finding the center of both the window and the template, and mark this on the countertop. Then measure from the lip of the countertop to the inside of the cabinet and transfer this to the countertop. This is where you'll position the front of the template; make sure to align it from side to side on the center marks you made earlier.

Prepare to cut. With the template temporarily held in place with tape, draw a line around it with a permanent marker. Then remove the template and drill one or more access holes near the corners for the saw blade you'll use to cut the opening.

Cut out the opening. A saber saw is the best choice for cutting out the opening. Insert the blade in one of the access holes and begin cutting the sides of the opening. Stop when you've cut both, and then screw a cleat temporarily across the width of the opening so the cleat ends rest on the countertop. This will support the cutout and prevent it from dropping into the cabinet as you complete the cuts.

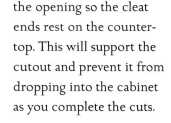

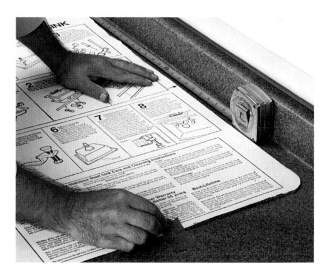

Seal the edges. Most countertops made with plastic laminate surfaces use particleboard for the substrate. Although particleboard is great for this since it's very flat and bonds well to laminate, it does have a problem with moisture. Unprotected particleboard will soak up water like a sponge. That's why it's a good idea to seal the edges of the opening with a couple of coats of latex paint. This is added insurance that if the seal under the sink fails, the countertop won't be damaged.

ENLARGING OR DECREASING A SINK OPENING

■ If you're replacing a sink but not the countertop, the new sink may or may not fit in the existing opening. As long as the difference between the two is less than $1/2$", you can use either technique shown here to enlarge or reduce the opening.

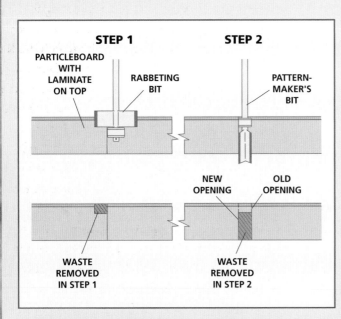

STEP 1   STEP 2

PARTICLEBOARD
WITH
LAMINATE
ON TOP
RABBETING
BIT

PATTERN-
MAKER'S
BIT

NEW
OPENING   OLD
OPENING

WASTE
REMOVED
IN STEP 1

WASTE
REMOVED
IN STEP 2

Enlarging an opening. The challenge to enlarging an opening just slightly is it's difficult to take just a bit off with a power saw with any kind of accuracy. Here's a slick way to do it with a router or laminate trimmer. Start by running a $1/4$" rabbeting bit around the perimeter of the opening. Then follow this up with a patternmaker's bit. The bearing of the patternmaker's bit will track along the rabbet you just cut to create an accurate larger opening.

ATTACH CLEATS
WITH EPOXY
AND NAILS

Reducing an opening. Reducing a sink opening is simple. Just attach cleats to the inside edges of the opening with epoxy and nails. The only critical thing here is to make sure the strips are thin enough to allow the new sink to fit in the new opening. To check this, make a trial run without epoxy and check the fit. If the sink fits, remove the strips and add the epoxy.

Undermount Sink

The advantage of an undermount sink is easy to see: There's no rim—just clean, smooth countertop. This means there's nothing for water to leak under and nothing to catch food particles. The only problem with undermount sinks is that they can be installed only in solid-surface countertops, where the edges of the openings are

waterproof. The plywood or particleboard edges of laminate countertops will not only look bad, but they're also easily damaged by moisture.

Fabricator-cut opening. Since solid-surface materials can be cut only by certified fabricators, you'll need the sink in advance of ordering the countertop so the fabricators can custom-cut an opening to fit the sink; they can also drill holes for

the faucet at the same time. When it's time to install the sink, they'll either drill holes underneath the sink around the opening and epoxy in threaded inserts for rim clips, or add cleats inside the cabinet for the sink to rest on. Either way, they'll apply a generous bead of silicone caulk around the sink rim and front edge of the cabinet. This is all the holding power needed, since the countertop is heavy enough to lock the sink in place.

UNDERMOUNT FASTENING SYSTEMS

■ Some undermount sink manufacturers have developed neat mounting systems that make it even easier to install their sinks. The system show here was developed by *Just Manufacturing* to simplify undermount installations. The system consists of a pair of tracks that are cut to fit across the depth of the cabinet. Channels inside each track accept square adjusting bolts that house screws; these screws, when tightened, force the rim of the sink up firmly against the underside of the countertop. The beauty of this system is that the adjusting bolts slide back and forth in the track to apply pressure wherever needed.

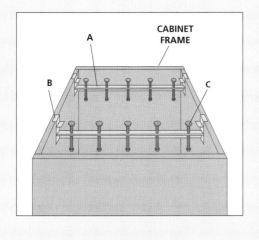

A   CABINET FRAME

B   C

Installing a Self-Rimming Sink

A new sink can give an instant facelift to a kitchen. What's more, replacing a kitchen sink is the perfect time to upgrade to a new material, a new style, or better features such as deeper bowls. The self-rimming stainless steel sink shown here is a kitchen classic. The term "self-rimming" simply means the lip or flange of the bowl overhangs the countertop. This in itself does not create a watertight seal. To achieve this, the sink requires a dozen or so small clips that hook onto a lip on the underside of the sink and pull the sink down tight against the countertop when the screws are tightened. This presses the bead of sealant or putty that's under the rim firmly against the countertop to prevent water from seeping under.

One of the nice things about many kitchen sinks is that they have been standardized to fit in precut holes in ready-made countertops. If you're installing a new countertop and sink, check to make sure they're made to fit together. If you're installing a sink in a new countertop where you'll have to cut an opening, or in an existing countertop where you need to enlarge or reduce an opening, follow the procedure on pages 157–158. In situations where you will just be replacing a sink, you'll first need to remove the old one; see pages 155–156 for step-by-step directions on how to do this.

Install faucet and strainers. It's easiest to install the sink faucet and strainers before installing the sink, as you have better access. Set the sink upside down on the countertop, protected by a towel or blanket, and slide it so it overhangs the countertop enough for you to insert the faucet set and strainers from underneath. Use the gasket supplied or plumber's putty to create a seal. Secure the faucet by tightening the mounting nuts; tighten the rings on the strainer to lock them in place. Remove any excess putty with a plastic putty knife.

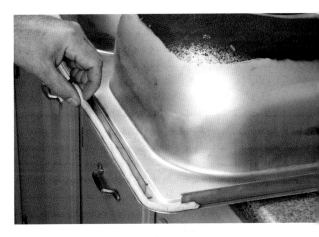

Add the sealant. Now you apply the sealant under the rim of the new sink. Apply a continuous, generous bead of silicone caulk or $1/2$"-diameter coil of plumber's putty around the rim. Alternatively, you can apply the sealant to the edge of the sink cutout. In either case, you should make sure the existing countertop is free of old putty or caulk by first wiping it down with mineral spirits or acetone.

Install new sink. Flip the sink right side up and position it in the opening. Center it from front to back and from side to side before pressing down to compress the sealant. Note that if you're installing a cast-iron sink, it's a good idea to temporarily place scraps of wood on each side of the opening and set the sink on these. Cast-iron sinks are heavy, and these wood scraps help prevent squished fingers.

Secure sink. With the sink in position, install the rim clips per the manufacturer's directions and tighten them to lock the sink in place (see page 155 for more on rim clips). Work alternate edges of the sink, tightening a clip on one side, then the clip opposite it. This helps ensure an even squeeze-out of the sealant.

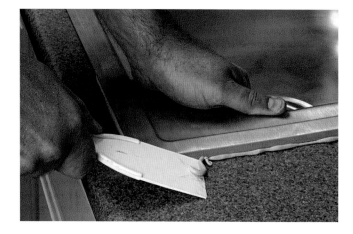

Remove any putty or caulk squeeze-out from around the rim with a plastic putty knife and then wipe off the sink and countertop with a clean, soft cloth.

Hook up supply lines. Now you can hook up the waste and supply lines. Because the waste line will block access to the supply lines, it's easier to hook up the supply lines first. Wrap a couple of turns of Teflon tape around the threads of the faucet supply openings and the shutoff valves. In most cases, you'll be connecting the faucet to

the valve with flexible supply lines (see page 154). When tight, remove the aerator from the faucet and test. Retighten as necessary to stop any leaks.

Hook up waste line. All that's left is to hook up the waste line. Typically this includes running tailpieces from each strainer, which are then connected together with either one or two elbows and a Y-connector. Chrome-plated brass fittings hold up better over time than PVC plastic fittings and are less susceptible to puncture.

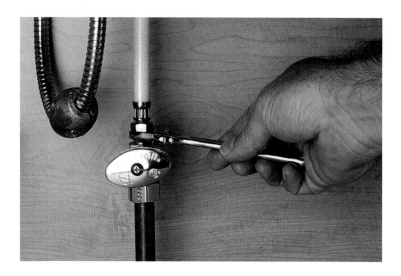

SNAP-IN SINKS

■ To make it easier to install sinks, a few innovative manufacturers of stainless-steel models have developed attachment systems that let you install the sink from the top. This eliminates groping around under the sink, fighting to tighten rim clips. The system shown here (patented by *Just Manufacturing*) features spring tension clips that attach to the sides of the opening. The clips mate with a special rolled metal lip under the rim to pull the sink down tight against the countertop.

Apply plumber's putty. To create a waterproof seal, run a bead of caulk or a coil of plumber's putty around the underside of the sink's rim before installing the sink.

Install clips. The first step is to attach the spring clips to the edges of the opening with the nails provided. Clips are attached 1" from each corner on all sides; the remainder are evenly spaced around the perimeter of the opening.

Snap sink in place. Next, just position the sink centered over the opening and set it down. Engage the clips by pressing the sink firmly in place. The faucet and strainers can be installed before the sink is snapped in place. Remove any caulk or putty squeeze-out with a plastic putty knife, and clean the sink and countertop with a soft cloth.

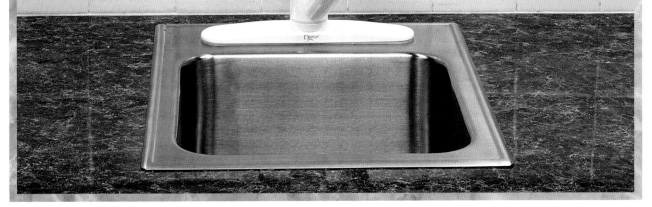

Solid-Surface Sink

Sinks that are manufactured from solid-surface materials let home-owners create countertops with a uniform, unbroken appearance. Solid-surface sinks may be self-rimming or more commonly, like the one shown here, are designed to be mounted under the sink, where they're attached with special adhesives. Most solid-surface sinks are white, but some colors are available at a slightly higher cost.

ACRYLIC SINK

Sink installation. As with any other solid-surface installation, a solid-surface sink must be attached by a certified fabricator who has access to the special adhesives required. You can cut down the time this will take by installing the strainers and faucet yourself in advance of the installation. Before you do this, check with the installers to make sure this won't be a problem. If it is, ask them to install these before placing the countertop—it's just a lot easier than crawling under a sink.

NO-LEAK SINK

■ Solid-surface sinks that are bonded to the underside of a countertop as shown here are about as close to leakproof as you can get. The special adhesives that fabricators use to attach the sink are formulated to actually fuse the parts together. Not only that, but the adhesives come in colors to match the sink and/or countertop so there's virtually no joint line—it's practically invisible.

Installing a New Faucet

TOOLS

- Basin wrench
- Adjustable wrench
- Putty knife
- Screwdriver

Although a simple job, replacing or upgrading an existing faucet does present a challenge. The challenge is accessing the parts—much like changing the oil filter in many cars. Because of the location of the faucet, you'll often end up on your back, reaching up behind the sink to loosen the

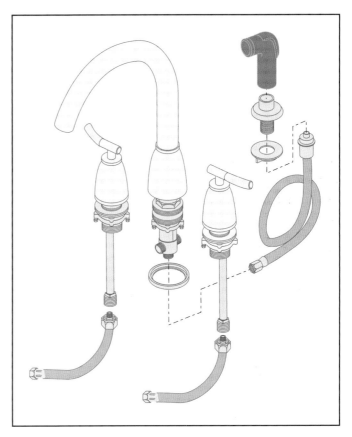

mounting nuts. At the same time you have to navigate past the supply and waste lines, working in an area that provides little, if any, elbow room. Fortunately, there's a handy tool called a basin wrench that can alleviate this problem; it's designed for one thing: removing and installing fixtures in sinks (see the sidebar on page 166).

Before you can remove your old faucet so it can be replaced, you'll need to turn off the water and disconnect its supply lines. If your sink has shutoff valves, turn them clockwise to shut off the water. If not, you'll need to turn off the main water lines. With the water off, use an adjustable wrench to loosen the nuts connecting the faucet supply lines to the shutoff valves or main water lines (see page 155 for more on this).

Remove mounting nuts. If you're working under the sink, here's where the basin wrench comes in. Position the jaws of the wrench around a mounting nut and turn the handle. If the nut doesn't loosen, give the handle a series of quick, hard turns to break it free. If after repeated efforts it still won't budge, you may have to disconnect the waste line and remove the sink for full access to these notoriously stubborn nuts. If applicable, disconnect the sprayer from the sink and faucet.

Remove old faucet. Before you remove the old faucet, it's a good idea to run the blade of a putty knife around its perimeter to sever the bond between the faucet and sink from the old caulk or plumber's putty. Even then, grasp the faucet firmly with both hands and pull up. The putty or caulk used to install the original faucet often develops a surprisingly strong bond over time.

BASIN WRENCH

■ A basin wrench is a specialty tool that's designed to let you reach up and loosen faucet nuts in close quarters. It has a long extension arm that lets you loosen or tighten faucet mounting nuts in the clear space below a sink. With access so limited, it's hard to adjust the wrench to fit the nut. That's why the serrated jaws of a basin wrench are self-adjusting—they close to fit around the nut as pressure is applied. You'll find basin wrenches wherever plumbing supplies are sold.

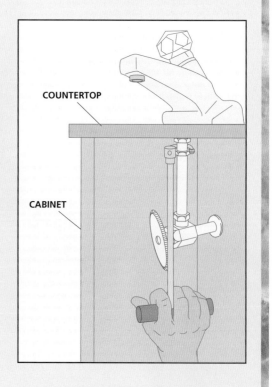

COUNTERTOP

CABINET

Prepare sink. Once you've pulled out the old faucet, it's important to remove any old putty or caulk from the sink. If you don't, you may not get a good seal under the new faucet. Use a putty knife to scrape away the bulk of the old sealant. Then clean the surface thoroughly with a soft rag and some denatured alcohol.

Install new faucet. Use the gasket provided with the new faucet. If possible, attach flexible supply lines to the faucet first, then set it in position and thread on the mounting nuts from underneath by hand; use the basin wrench to finish tightening the mounting nuts if you're working from under the sink. Wrap fresh Teflon tape around the threads of the shutoff valves of the water supply lines, and tighten the connecting nuts with an adjustable wrench.

Connect valves if necessary. Unlike its one-piece cousin, a wide-spread faucet like the one shown here has several parts, typically a spout, separate handles, and options such as a sprayer. These faucets can be installed in any sink designed for a one-piece faucet. On most, a T-connector hooked up to the spout accepts hot and cold water from valves installed beneath the

faucet handles. Other systems run hot and cold water directly into the handle, which then routes the mixture off to the spout via a flexible line.

Installing a Pullout Sprayer Unit

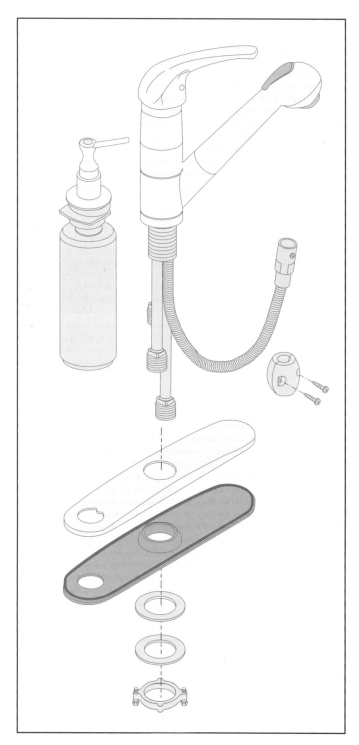

TOOLS

- Adjustable wrench
- Screwdriver
- Basin wrench (optional)

Pullout sprayer faucets are all the rage…and for good reason. By combining a sprayer and a faucet in one, they free up holes in the sink or countertop so you can add other accessories, like a soap dispenser or instant hot-water dispenser. They also have the added benefit of providing spray action at the touch of a button. Pullout sprayer faucets are installed much the same way as a standard faucet (see pages 165–167), but with a few peculiarities.

the sprayer (taking care not to let go of its hose) before running water through the unit for the first time, to protect it from debris in the lines.

Attach counterweight. The final thing you'll find different with pullout sprayers is that they need a counterweight to be attached to the sprayer hose to pull the hose back into the faucet body once it's been extended. The counterweight is usually a pair of lead weights that are split to wrap around the hose and are screwed together. Take care to tighten them only friction-tight, as you could restrict water flow by overtightening.

Insert faucet in sink. In most pullout sprayer faucets, the faucet body is first installed in the sink and tightened in place, then the sprayer hose is threaded through the body and attached to the base. On some faucets, like the one shown here, this isn't necessary, and all you need do is thread the unit through the opening in the sink or countertop.

Aerator or filter location. Another difference on these faucets is that unlike a standard faucet, where the aerator threads onto the end of the spout, the aerator on many pullout units is located between the sprayer and its connecting hose. Other pullout sprayers use this location to house a filter that prevents debris from clogging the sprayer. In either case, you should remove

KITCHEN ELECTRICAL

There's nothing ho-hum about power in the kitchen. Your electrical system backs every "on" button in the room, from the microwave to the wall oven to the under-cabinet lighting. Electricity vents away unpleasant odors, washes the dishes, grinds in-sink garbage, and tells you when the roast is done. There are some electrical projects that are best left to professionals, but if you're comfortable working with electricity, there are many jobs you can do yourself. We'll look at the safe and smart ways to accomplish everything from installing ground-fault circuit interrupters (GFCIs) to wiring a dishwasher.

An often-overlooked aspect of kitchen electricals that makes a huge difference in design success is lighting. You can highlight an island with pendant lamps, accent crown molding with recessed lights, or use under-cabinet lights for evening ambience. What you can't do easily, though, is manage lighting jobs without access to the ceiling from above. If you don't have access, consider using a pro: Wiring will need to be snaked through walls, floors, and ceilings.

Installing GFCIs

GFCI receptacles are safety devices designed to detect small variations in current flow between the two legs of a circuit. When an imbalance (or short circuit) occurs, the GFCI will shut off the power to the receptacle almost instantaneously. Most building codes specify that receptacles in the kitchen be ground-fault-protected. Replacing a standard receptacle with a GFCI is simple, since it's just a matter of hooking up the new receptacle to the existing wiring.

Remove old receptacle. To install a GFCI receptacle, start by turning off and tagging power at the main service panel. Then check the existing outlet with a circuit tester to make sure power is

indeed off. Remove the cover plate screw and cover plate. Unscrew the receptacle-mounting screws and set them aside. Gently pull out the old receptacle, loosen each of the screw terminals, and unhook all of the wires.

Install GFCI. Now you can connect the wires to the appropriate screw terminals (or wires) of the GFCI receptacle. If this is a single-protection receptacle, attach the pigtailed wires

to the screw terminals labeled LINE. For multiple-location protection (see the sidebar below), connect the incoming wires to the LINE terminal screws, and the line to be protected to the screw terminals labeled LOAD. Connect the ground wire to the receptacle, push the receptacle back into the box, and secure it with mounting screws. Add the cover plate and screw, and restore power.

PROTECTING MULTIPLE OUTLETS

■ Most GFCI receptacles can be wired to protect just themselves or to protect all wiring, switches, and light fixtures forward of the GFCI receptacle to the end of the circuit. GFCI receptacles are safest and most reliable when wired for single protection. Multiple-location protection is susceptible to erroneous tripping when normal fluctuations occur—which can be very annoying because you have to reset the circuit every time this happens. If you must wire a GFCI to protect multiple locations, follow the manufacturer's directions carefully (or have a licensed electrician do the work). Miswiring can leave both the outlet and the line you intend to protect without any ground-fault protection.

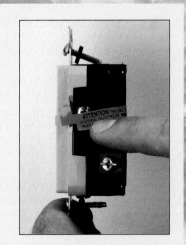

Under-Cabinet Lighting

TOOLS

- Screwdriver
- Electric drill
- Hammer (optional)

If you have an older kitchen, chances are that all the artificial light in the room comes from a single overhead fixture and a stove light. Although there's probably a window, it lets in light during the day only, and probably just around the sink. As a result, there isn't any light where you really need it—at the counters where you do food preparation. The solution to this common problem is to install under-cabinet lighting, lighting that mounts in a strip arrangement underneath the overhead cabinets.

Most manufacturers recommend locating the strip as close to the front of the cabinet as possible to create the best coverage. Locate and mark the holes for the mounting hardware; drill pilot holes for the screws (provided with most lights), and then drive the screws into the bottom of the cabinet.

Finally, install the strip and plug it in. Fluorescent fixtures can plug right into a receptacle; halogen fixtures usually require a low-voltage transformer. Note: If the light strip is visible at eye level, install a valance strip to hide the light and prevent glare. This strip is just a 1" to 2" strip of wood nailed to the front edge and finished to match the cabinet.

PUCK-STYLE LIGHTS

■ Some areas in the kitchen may not need an entire strip of lights. Here's where small, individual hockey-puck-shaped halogen lights are ideal. Puck lights are available in packs of two or more and can be mounted exactly where you need the light and then wired together. Wiring is simple: The wiring just snaps into each light. The final puck in the string is connected to a low-voltage transformer, which is plugged into a nearby receptacle.

Installing Recessed Lighting

TOOLS

- Stubby screwdriver
- Circuit tester
- Cutter/stripper
- Drywall saw and compass
- Needlenose pliers

Recessed lights in the kitchen offer a number of advantages over other lighting choices. They're easy to install, they let you put light exactly where you need it, and, because they're recessed into the ceiling, they give the impression of higher ceilings. Another plus: These lights are so unobtrusive, they're guaranteed not to clash or interfere with the other kitchen design elements.

Most recessed lights are designed to be mounted in one of three situations: in suspended ceilings, in new construction, and, the one that applies most to makeovers, in remodel work. The first step in installing a recessed light in an existing kitchen is to identify where you want the lights. Then locate the ceiling joists. If you have easy access to the ceiling from above, you can secure the fixture to the joists (see the drawing below). When access is restricted, you'll use the remodel clips provided with the light (see page 175).

If possible, locate the light between joists to

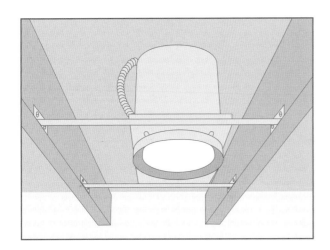

provide plenty of clearance during installation. Use a compass to mark the hole for the light on the ceiling and cut it out with a drywall, saber, or reciprocating saw. Then run power to the light; the simplest way to do this is to route the power cable of the old overhead light to the new location. That way the existing light switch can control the lights. If this isn't possible, run new lines or have them installed by an electrician. (Note: If your ceiling is insulated, as most are, make sure to purchase lights that are rated to come in contact with insulation.)

Separate parts and hook up wiring.

Most remodel recessed lights have two main parts: a mounting frame and a "can." Separating the parts allows you to install the light from below (photos at right). Remove the screws as directed, and drop the can through the frame. Then, making sure the power is off to the light, route the electrical cable into the junction box on the frame and connect the wires as directed.

Insert frame in ceiling and attach clips.

Now you can insert the junction box and frame into the hole in the ceiling and secure it with the remodel clips provided. These spring clips hold the frame in place by gripping the sides of the frame and pressing up against the ceiling. They'll hold the frame in place until the installation is complete (photos below left).

Push in can and add trim.

All that's left is to insert the can up into the frame and secure it with the screws provided. You'll need either a

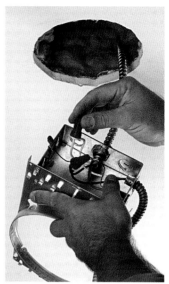

"stubby" screwdriver or a small socket wrench to tighten these, as space inside the can is cramped. Once secured, you can attach the trim. In most cases, it attaches to the inside of the can with a set of springs. Needlenose pliers are your best bet here. Finally, insert a lightbulb, restore power, and test.

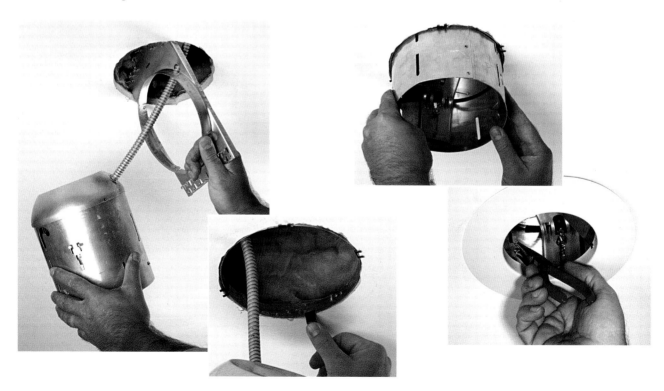

Installing Pendant Lights

TOOLS

- Screwdriver
- Circuit tester
- Cutter/stripper
- Drywall saw and compass
- Needlenose pliers

Lights that hang down from the ceiling—pendant lights—are perfect for lighting islands and peninsulas in the kitchen. And because they'll be highly visible, they can really add to the design of the kitchen. You can choose a style that blends well with the design and is less noticeable, or one that stands out as an accent. Either way, there are two basic versions of a pendant light: one where the light is suspended simply by its electrical cord, and, like the one shown here, one where the light is suspended via a metal rod that hides the electrical cord.

Whichever you choose, installation is very similar. As with recessed lighting, your first step is to identify where you want the pendant lights and then to locate the ceiling joists. Then use a compass to mark the hole and cut it out with a drywall, saber, or reciprocating saw. Now you can run power to the location. If possible, it's easiest to route the existing switch-controlled light cable to the new light. Since pendant lights can be heavy, it's best to install electrical boxes that attach to hangers that span the joists (see the illustration below). These special hanger-style boxes are designed for below-ceiling installation. The two-part hanger is fed up through the ceiling hole, the ends of the bars are extended to contact the joists, and then the hanger is expanded (usually via a threaded nut) until the prongs on the ends of the hanger bite into the joists.

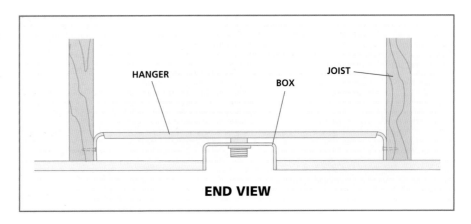

HANGER   BOX   JOIST

END VIEW

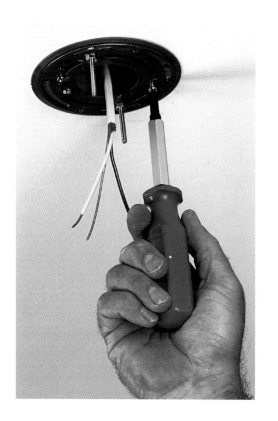

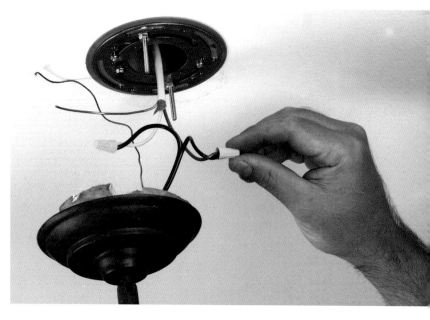

Attach mounting plate. Once you've installed the hanger box and routed the electrical line, the next step is to install the mounting plate provided with the light. This plate serves as a transition between the box and the cover of the light. Attach it to the box with the screws provided, and route the electrical cable through the opening in the center of the plate.

Make power connections. Now you can connect the electrical cable to the wires of the light. Before you do this, inspect the wire coming out of the box. If the insulation is cracked or the ends are nicked or tarnished, cut the ends off and strip off ½" of the insulation from the end with a wire stripper. Then attach the new fixture wires to the circuit wires with wire nuts that are supplied with the new fixture.

Mount the light. All that's left is to mount the pendant itself. Start by pushing any exposed wiring up and into the electrical box. Most covers are held in place with decorative nuts that screw onto rods that thread into the mounting plate. Align the cover of the light so its holes are directly over the rods, and push up until the rods poke through; then thread on the decorative nuts. Install bulbs, restore power, and test.

Installing a Cooktop

TOOLS

- Screwdriver
- Circuit tester
- Cutter/stripper
- Saber saw

Ever since ovens began being installed separately from the cooktop, stand-alone cooktops have been growing in popularity. They're especially well suited for installation in islands (and peninsulas, as shown here). The use of the space below the cooktop will depend on the type of venting chosen. For overhead range hoods, this area now becomes storage—always desirable. If a downdraft vent system (or telescoping downdraft system, like the one shown on page 182) is used, the space is likely to be taken up with the vent unit, or remote blower.

Cut out opening. In either case, installing the actual cooktop is quite simple. All you need do is use the manufacturer's template to mark the location of the opening for the cooktop on the countertop and cut it out. This procedure is almost identical to cutting an opening for a sink (see pages 157–158 for more on this). For a solid-surface countertop, the fabricator will need to cut the opening.

Attach hardware and install cooktop.

Most cooktops attach to the countertop with some type of special mounting hardware. The modular Gaggenau cooktop shown here snaps into brackets that are attached to the edges of the countertop. In laminate countertops, these brackets are screwed in place; for solid-surface tops, they are glued to the edges with special heat-resistant epoxy. With the mounting hardware in place, position the cooktop and press down to lock it in place. Other types may require locking the cooktop in place from under the cabinet.

Installing a Wall Oven

TOOLS

- Screwdriver
- Circular or hand saw
- Electric drill

Whoever invented the wall oven saved the backs of cooks around the world. Although some might feel that this is a waste of wall and/or cabinet space, anyone who has cooked with one will tell you it's wonderful. No more bending over to see if the cookies are done—they're in plain sight. And back strain from lifting a heavy roast or bird out of a standard oven has gone away as well.

Build support rack. Wall ovens are becoming so popular that most cabinet manufacturers now offer tall cabinets specifically designed to house wall ovens. The only problem is, they don't offer any kind of internal framework to support the oven. This makes sense since there's such variety of wall oven types and sizes. So before you can install your wall oven, you'll need to build a simple frame out of scrap wood for it to rest on. You'll also need a suitable electrical receptacle to plug it in behind the oven, and a gas line if it heats with gas. Running electrical and gas lines is best left to professionals.

Slide in unit and secure. With the support rack built and the power (and gas if necessary) run to the oven, you can slide the unit into the cabinet. Depending on the width of your oven and the cabinet, you may first need to install filler strips on each side of the oven to eliminate gaps between the oven and cabinet sides. Hook up the oven and then slide it in place; then secure it to the cabinet with the screws provided and test it.

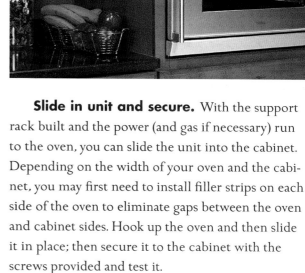

Installing a Range Hood

TOOLS

- Screwdriver or nutdriver
- Tape measure
- Electric drill
- Slip-joint pliers
- Circuit tester
- Cutter/stripper
- Compass
- Needlenose pliers
- Saber and drywall saws

There is a byproduct of good cooking that's both good and bad—the aroma. Yes, the smell of garlic roasting, bacon frying, or soup simmering can be wonderful. But if the smells are left to linger, they can both offend the senses and deposit moisture and grease over your appliances, cabinets, countertops, and flooring. The solution to this dilemma is a range hood.

Install side cleats if necessary. If you're replacing an existing range hood (as we're doing here), start by turning off power to the hood. Then disconnect the power, loosen the mounting screws, and remove the old hood. Depending on the location of the

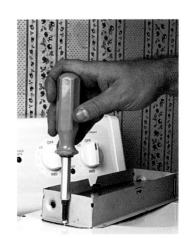

mounting holes in the new hood, you may need to attach cleats to the undersides of the cabinet so the screws have something to drive into. If necessary, cut cleats to fit and screw them to the cabinet sides.

Prepare hood and cabinet. Before you can install the new hood, there's some prep work to be done on the hood and the cabinet. Start by removing the punch-out in the top of the hood for the louver (this is left in place for unvented hoods). Temporarily hold the range hood in position and trace the outline of the punch-out on the bottom of the cabinet. Then remove the hood, attach the louver, and cut out the opening for the louver in the cabinet with a saber saw or a reciprocating saw.

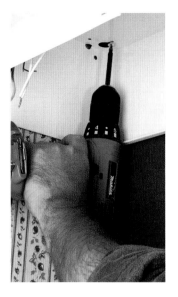

Install hood and hook up electrical.

Place the range hood back under the cabinet and mark the locations for the mounting holes. Remove the hood and drill pilot holes in the cabinet (or cleat, if you installed one). Now replace the range hood, making sure to route the electrical cable into the junction box, and drive in the mounting screws to secure the range hood to the cabinet.

Next connect the electrical line to the wires in the range hood, matching up colors: black wire to black wire, white to white, and green to green.

Install ducting.

Now for the fun part: running the ductwork. Most range hoods use one of two types of ducting (see the sidebar below). Whichever type you use, you'll have to make cutouts in the cabinet, ceiling, and soffit. The best way to do this is to start at the louver and attach the first piece of ductwork. Continue routing ducting until you hit an obstruction. Then use the actual ducting as a template and draw the cutout on the obstruction. Cut out the opening, insert the ducting, and continue until you've reached the soffit.

Here you'll need to terminate it with a spring-load vent to keep out vermin. Make sure to seal around the exterior vent with silicone caulk.

TYPES OF DUCTING

■ The two common types of ducting you'll find for range hoods are 6" round and 3"×10" rectangular. Since they both handle the same volume of air, they work equally well. The advantage of round ducting is that you can cut the opening with a large-diameter hole saw. Better yet, flexible round ducting is available that makes it a whole lot easier to route. Just make sure that it's rigid ducting and not the plastic hose commonly used for dryer vents, which would quickly melt from the high-temperature air flowing through it. Rectangular ducting is less forgiving than round is during installation, but it tends to hold up better over time.

Installing Downdraft Ventilation

TOOLS

- Screwdriver
- Tape measure
- Circuit tester
- Cutter/stripper
- Saber saw
- Electric drill and hole saw
- Caulk gun

Downdraft ventilation is perfect for those kitchens where you don't want a range hood as the focal point of the kitchen. These are particularly useful in smaller kitchens, where a large range hood would be obtrusive. Installing a downdraft unit is similar to installing a vented range hood (see pages 180–181). The big difference is that instead of running the ductwork up through the ceiling and out the soffitt, you route it down through the floor and out an exterior wall (see the illustration on page 183). Going through an exterior wall isn't mandatory—you could route the ducting up through an interior wall, through the ceiling, and out the roof—but going through the floor and out a wall is usually a lot more simple.

Downdraft ventilation units can have an integral blower or a remote blower. The advantage of a remote blower is that you can locate it away from the kitchen—even on the exterior wall—so that the ventilator seems virtually silent. This is quite a nice change from some range hoods that sound like aircraft taking off. The downside to remote blowers is that they're expensive and can be a challenge to install (see the sidebar on page 184 for more on this).

Cutouts for ducting. The tricky part to installing downdraft ventilation is accurately locating and then cutting out the openings for the ductwork in both the cabinet and the flooring underneath. One way to do this is to place the unit in the cabinet and mark the bottom of the cabinet by tracing around the exhaust port. If you're using round ducting (as we did here), you can cut the openings with a large-diameter hole saw (bottom photo). But before you do this, it's a good idea to drill a small pilot hole centered on the opening through both the cabinet base and the flooring. This ensures that the two holes will align.

Rout ducting through cabinet and floor. Once the holes are cut, attach a length of ducting to the exhaust port of the ventilator. (We used the flexible noncorrosive aluminum ducting recommended by the manufacturer.) Then position the ventilator in the opening in the countertop and guide the ducting through the holes in the cabinet and floor (top photos). An extra set of hands here will make this job much easier.

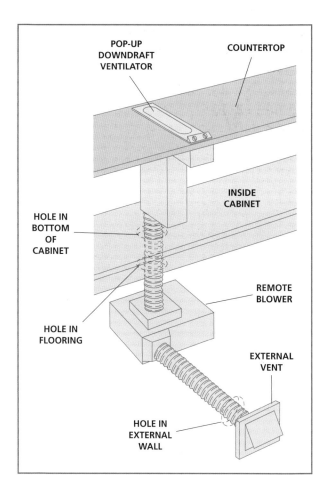

POP-UP DOWNDRAFT VENTILATOR

COUNTERTOP

INSIDE CABINET

HOLE IN BOTTOM OF CABINET

REMOTE BLOWER

HOLE IN FLOORING

EXTERNAL VENT

HOLE IN EXTERNAL WALL

Drill through exterior wall. Once the ducting is run through the floor, it can be connected to the exterior vent or, as in our case, connected to the remote blower. In either case, the ducting then needs to exit through an exterior wall. Try to keep the ducting as short as possible and limit turns as much as possible; manufacturers provide guidelines with the installation instructions. Locate the best place to exit the exterior wall, and cut an opening with a reciprocating saw or hole saw.

Install vent cap. All that's left is to install a spring-loaded vent cap in the exterior wall and connect the ducting to it. Round ducting is usually connected with hose clamps; rectangular ducting, with pop rivets. Before you insert the vent cap through the opening, apply a generous bead of silicone around the back of the vent that'll come in contact with the wall. This, along with a bead of silicone around the installed cap, will provide an excellent seal. If your exterior wall covering permits, secure the vent cap with screws; otherwise the silicone will suffice.

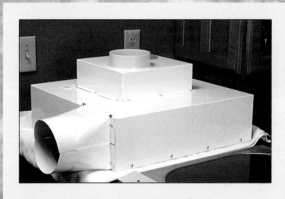

REMOTE BLOWERS

■ When more and more cooks complained about noisy range hoods, a couple of savvy manufacturers responded by offering remote blowers like the one shown here. Although remote blowers do offer much quieter operation, they can contribute significantly to the cost of the ventilation system. That's because it's more expensive to manufacture the blower separately, and a lot more expensive to install it. Installation is expensive because a remote unit requires its own power connections, and a cable must be run between the cooktop and the blower so it'll activate when the fan switch on the cooktop is engaged.

Installing a Garbage Disposal

TOOLS

- Screwdriver
- Tape measure
- Circuit tester
- Cutter/stripper
- Electric drill
- Adjustable wrench
- Slip-joint and needlenose pliers

Installing a garbage disposal isn't something you'll often see as part of a makeover, but it's an excellent feature to add to your kitchen. And, there's no better time to run the electrical line and switch for a disposal than when cabinets are removed and walls will be redone. Since installing a disposal requires both plumbing and electrical skills, it's a project for an experienced do-it-yourselfer. One way to simplify the task is to have a licensed electrician install a countertop switch and a GFCI receptacle under the sink. Then the electrical work left for you is to wire a power cord to the disposal and plug it in. Note: Before you get started with the installation, you'll find you have better access under the sink if you temporarily remove the cabinet doors and set them aside.

the disposal will fit under your sink. Measure from the bottom of the sink to the bottom of the cabinet. Then check the required clearance noted on the box before you buy your disposal.

Remove waste line and strainer. To install a disposal in an existing sink, start by disconnecting the old waste line. (If you're installing the disposal in a new sink, skip to the next step.) Position a bucket under the trap and have rags handy for spills. Loosen the compression nuts on the trap first and remove it. Then remove the tailpiece from the sink. Depending on your disposal, you may or may not be able to reuse these parts. Next, loosen the ring that secures the strainer and remove the strainer. Although strainer wrenches are available, you can loosen the strainer by inserting the jaws of a set of needlenose pliers in the holes in the strainer; twist to loosen the ring. Once removed, clean off any old putty around the opening.

Install flange. Now you're ready to install the disposal. Remove the mounting assembly by loosening the flange screws and popping off a snap ring that holds the flange in place. Then remove the flange and apply plumber's putty around the opening in the sink before setting it in place.

Check installation dimensions. Since disposals vary greatly in size, and bowl depth varies from sink to sink, it's important to check the installation dimensions to make sure

screws. Thread the screws up far enough so the mounting flange is friction-tight and then slowly tighten each screw, alternating among them so you end up with evenly applied pressure.

Mount disposal. The disposal attaches to the sink with the mounting assembly. Lift the disposal up so the ring on the top of the disposal mates with the mounting assembly. Then turn the ring so it pulls the disposal up snug to the bottom of the assembly. Most disposals include a special wrench (similar to an Allen wrench) that fits in rolled loops in the ring so you can tighten the ring with some leverage.

Snap in upper mounting assembly. The next step is one of those tasks where you'll wish you had three hands. While holding down the sink flange from above (either enlist the aid of a helper or use a heavy weight for this), slip the mounting assembly up onto the flange. Then stretch the snap ring over the flange and push it up until it's forced over the lip that will keep it (and the mounting assembly) from slipping off.

Tighten upper mounting assembly. To lock the mounting assembly in place and pull the flange down to provide a good seal in the sink opening, tighten the three flange

Attach discharge tube. To get the disposal ready to hook up to your waste line, first attach the discharge tube with the screws provided. Next, prepare the dishwasher drain connection if you'll be connecting the disposal to your dishwasher. This usually entails knocking out a drain plug and attaching the drain hose from the dishwasher.

Connect to waste line. If necessary, loosen the disposal's ring slightly. You want to be able to rotate the disposal so that the discharge tube aligns with the drain trap. If your sink is a double bowl, you'll need to re-plumb the waste line to attach to the disposal. If you're lucky, all you'll need is an extension tube. If not, you may need to replace the entire waste line all the way back to the P-trap.

Connect to electrical supply.
Finally, connect the disposal to power. Wire the recommended grounded electrical cord to the disposal and plug it into the receptacle. Since there's both water and electrical power present there, it's best to

install a ground-fault-protected receptacle (see page 172 for more on this). Check your local code if you're in doubt as to whether or not this is required.

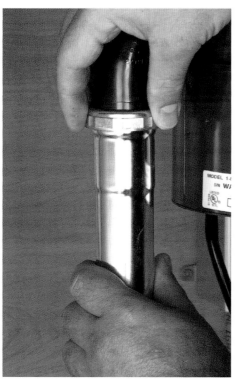

Installing a Dishwasher

TOOLS

- Circuit tester
- Cutter/stripper
- Adjustable wrench
- Screwdriver
- Electric drill

Like a garbage disposal, installing a dishwasher requires both plumbing and electrical skills. Fortunately, the tasks involved in each area are fairly simple. Most dishwashers require only a 110-volt line. Some plug into a receptacle; others are hard-wired. The plumbing tasks are equally easy. You'll need to run a hot water line to the dishwasher and provide a drain for it. The hot water line can be tapped under the sink; the drain issue can be solved by adding a new tailpiece, one equipped with a dishwasher drain inlet.

Since dishwasher installation varies greatly from one manufacturer to another, it's important to read and follow their directions. In some areas, local code requires that all dishwasher installations include the installation of an air gap. An air gap is a device that "breaks" the waste line to prevent wastewater from back-siphoning into the dishwasher; most are designed for mounting in the extra hole commonly found in stainless-steel sinks.

Hook up the plumbing. To prepare for the installation of the dishwasher, start by branching off the hot water line under the sink with a T-fitting. It's well worth the effort to add a separate shutoff valve for this line, which will make future maintenance and repair much easier. Next, replace your existing sink's tailpiece with one ready to accept a dishwasher drain. Run the supply line from the dishwasher and connect it to the shutoff valve; route the drain line to the tailpiece, slide it on the inlet, and secure it with the hose clamp that's provided.

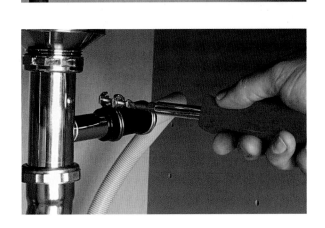

Slide in unit and secure.

Before you slide the dishwasher into the cabinet, remove the access panel at the front of the dishwasher. The panel is located near the bottom and is typically secured with a pair of screws. Located behind the panel are the connec-

tion for the hot water supply and the junction box for the electrical hookup. Make sure to route these two lines under the dishwasher as per the manufacturer's directions. Then slide the unit into the cabinet and level it according to the directions. Secure the dishwasher either to the underside of the countertop or to the sides of the cabinet (as shown here).

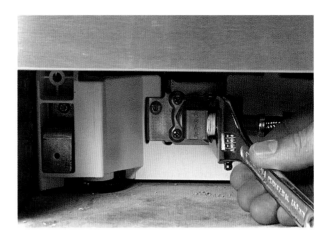

Hook up hot water line. With the dishwasher in place, you can hook up the hot water supply line. This is usually terminated with an L-fitting that threads onto a nipple (photo above). Wrap a few turns of Teflon tape around the threads and then tighten the fitting with an adjustable wrench. Turn on the hot water line and check for leaks; retighten or repair as needed.

Make electrical connections. Finally, hook the electrical line up to the dishwasher. Make sure power is off, and connect the wires with wire nuts (photo below). When finished, replace the access panel and secure it with the screws you removed earlier. Turn on the dishwasher and test, making sure the drain connections are watertight.

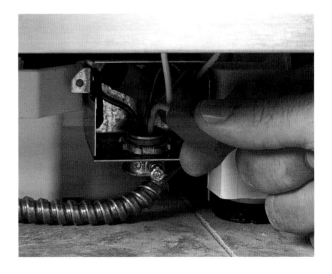

Index

METRIC EQUIVALENCY CHART

Inches to millimeters and centimeters

inches	mm	cm	inches	cm	inches	cm
1/8	3	0.3	9	22.9	30	76.2
1/4	6	0.6	10	25.4	31	78.7
3/8	10	1.0	11	27.9	32	81.3
1/2	13	1.3	12	30.5	33	83.8
5/8	16	1.6	13	33.0	34	86.4
3/4	19	1.9	14	35.6	35	88.9
7/8	22	2.2	15	38.1	36	91.4
1	25	2.5	16	40.6	37	94.0
1 1/4	32	3.2	17	43.2	38	96.5
1 1/2	38	3.8	18	45.7	39	99.1
1 3/4	44	4.4	19	48.3	40	101.6
2	51	5.1	20	50.8	41	104.1
2 1/2	64	6.4	21	53.3	42	106.7
3	76	7.6	22	55.9	43	109.2
3 1/2	89	8.9	23	58.4	44	111.8
4	102	10.2	24	61.0	45	114.3
4 1/2	114	11.4	25	63.5	46	116.8
5	127	12.7	26	66.0	47	119.4
6	152	15.2	27	68.6	48	121.9
7	178	17.8	28	71.1	49	124.5
8	203	20.3	29	73.7	50	127.0

mm = millimeters   cm = centimeters